Empathy

Key Concepts in Philosophy

Empathy

Derek Matravers

polity

First published in 2017 by Polity Press

Polity Press
65 Bridge Street
Cambridge CB2 1UR, UK

Polity Press
350 Main Street
Malden, MA 02148, USA

ISBN-13: 978-0-7456-7074-4
ISBN-13: 978-0-7456-7075-1(pb)

A catalogue record for this book is available from the British Library.

Library of Congress Cataloging-in-Publication Data

Names: Matravers, Derek, author.
Title: Empathy / Derek Matravers.
Description: Malden, MA : Polity Press, 2017. | Includes bibliographical
 references and index.
Identifiers: LCCN 2016027668 | ISBN 9780745670744 (hardback : alk.
 paper) | ISBN 9780745670751 (pbk. : alk. paper)
Subjects: LCSH: Empathy. | Caring.
Classification: LCC BJ1475 .M426 2016 | DDC 177/.7–dc23 LC record
 available at https://lccn.loc.gov/2016027668

Typeset in 10.5 on 12 pt Sabon
by Toppan Best-set Premedia Limited
Printed and bound in the UK by Clays Ltd, St Ives PLC

For further information on Polity, visit our website: politybooks.com

For Amy Coplan

Contents

Acknowledgements

My thinking about empathy has been helped by my being a member of the International Network on Empathy, Sympathy, and the Imagination (INSEI). The network has benefitted from a British Academy/Leverhulme grant, which has enabled us to meet more regularly, the results of which have influenced what can be found in these pages. In addition to Louise Braddock, Louise Gyler, Katherine Harloe, Holly High, Michael Lacewing, Riana Betzler, Carolyn Price, Talia Morag and Adam Leite, I would like to give particular thanks to Anik Waldow, Katy Abramson and Maarten Steenhagen, who read sections of the manuscript. I would also like to thank Emma Hutchinson, Pascal Porcheron and Ellen MacDonald-Kramer at Polity, and the anonymous reviewers whose incisive comments did much to improve the book.

This book is a long-delayed addition to a project on empathy led by Amy Coplan and Peter Goldie. A conference, held in Fullerton in 2006, led to their seminal edited collection, *Empathy: Philosophical and Psychological Perspectives* (Oxford University Press, 2011). I had a hand in this, at least to the extent of introducing Amy and Peter at the first of a succession of meetings, both intellectual and social, that somehow managed to lift both philosophy and life to a better level. Peter died in 2011; in writing this book I have been reminded of my debt to him, which is reflected (however inadequately) on every page. I have dedicated the book, with a great deal of affection and respect, to Amy, fully conscious that she will find most of it completely wrong-headed.

The final draft of the book was written during a two-month period of leave which I spent in Las Palmas, Gran Canaria. For their fabulous hospitality, I would like to thank Colm, Lourdes, Sinéad and Aislinn. And, of course, the trip would not have been the same without my wife, Jane, for whom, I suspect, I present a limiting case for the claims that follow. Without her love and support life would not be nearly as splendid as in fact it is.

1
Introduction: Some Historical Preliminaries

'Empathy' is one of the catchwords of our time. In the course of his political career, Barack Obama has repeatedly called on people to address what he sees as 'an empathy deficit'; an inability or an unwillingness to see the world from the perspective of those less fortunate than ourselves. People who are training to be doctors are required to show empathy to patients, or, at least, those playing the role of patients for the purposes of examinations (Jamison 2014: Ch. 1). There are international movements dedicated to the cultivation of empathy, an online empathy library, empathy classes in schools, and a recent book has claimed that empathy is 'a key to a global and social revolution' (Krznaric 2014). Furthermore, the range of human endeavour in which empathy features is impressive. It is prominent within philosophy: it features in the philosophy of mind and the philosophy of history, ethics and aesthetics. It has a key role in the human sciences, particularly within what is known as 'the phenomenological tradition'. Within psychology, it has a place in developmental psychology, social psychology and clinical psychology. It also features increasingly in the developing cognitive sciences.

As we shall see, 'empathy' is a term used to cover a fascinating range of disparate phenomena. To enable us to set out on our journey around these phenomena I will venture a broad characterization: empathy is *using our imaginations as a tool so as to adopt a different perspective in order to grasp how things appear (or feel) from there.* Even such a broad characterization as this will be controversial; in particular, it does not include any reference to caring about, or helping, the person who is the object of the empathic engagement. In this, it contrasts with another recent attempt to gesture at the general area: an emotion is empathetic if the person who feels it 'is aware that it is caused by the perceived, imagined, or inferred emotion or plight of another, or it expresses concern for the welfare of another' (Maibom 2014: 2). However, if this catches the link to an interest in the welfare of another, it does so at the expense of not covering at least some of the recent debates in the philosophy of mind. We shall examine the similarities and differences between these conceptions of the topic as the book progresses. As we need to start somewhere, for the moment I will let them stand as rough characterizations of what I will be talking about.

It comes as something of a surprise to those who do not know, that the English word 'empathy' was coined as late as 1909. It is worth a brief historical digression to discover how this came about. In looking at the historical roots of empathy, we need to distinguish the history of the phenomenon from the history of the specific term. As for the phenomenon, I assume that people have been able to imagine themselves into another perspective (whether the perspective of themselves in a different time and/or space or the perspective of another person) for as long as people have been able to think. The phenomenon surfaced as being of some particular philosophical use in the work of David Hume and (more particularly) Adam Smith in the eighteenth century. Both Hume and Smith used the idea of sharing others' mental states as part of their explanation of morality. Of course, they did not have our term, but their term, 'sympathy', clearly describes something in the same area. Here is a famous passage from Hume in the *Treatise*:

> We may begin by considering a-new the nature and force of *sympathy*. The minds of all men are similar in their feelings and operations, nor can anyone be actuated by any affection, of which all others are not, in some degree, susceptible. As in strings equally wound up, the motion of one communicates itself to the rest; so all the affections readily pass from one person to the other, and beget correspondent movements in

every human creature. When I see the *effects* of passion in the voice and gesture of any person, my mind immediately passes from these effects to their causes, and forms such a lively idea of the passion, as is presently converted to the passion itself. In like manner, when I perceive the *causes* of any emotion, my mind is convey'd to the effects, and is actuated with a like emotion. (Hume 1739–40: III.iii.i)

In this passage, Hume is talking in particular about a passion (an emotion) passing from one person to another. He mentions two different ways in which this might happen. The first way, 'as in strings equally wound up, the motion of one communicates itself to the rest', looks to be a simple case of what is called 'emotional contagion', our 'catching' emotions from other people. For example, being in the company of happy people can make us happy, or being in the company of anxious people can make us anxious. We shall examine this in greater detail in the next chapter. The second way, in which 'my mind immediately passes from these effects to their causes, and forms such a lively idea of the passion, as is presently converted to the passion itself', looks slightly more complicated. In the *Treatise* Hume's account of psychology largely works by association. If, in the world, one thing is causally related to some other thing, then a thought about the first thing will tend to be followed by a thought about the second thing. The same is true if the objects are related by resemblance or contiguity in time and place. These associative links guide our thoughts, which suggests that, as with emotional contagion, the mind 'passing' from one mental state to another does not break into our conscious awareness. That is, I do not make conscious inferences from others' appearance and behaviour regarding how they feel, and then consciously get myself to feel the same; rather, it happens automatically. In Hume's later work, the *Enquiries*, his associationism is largely set to one side in favour of a focus on our actual processes of evaluation, which takes him closer to modern debates.[1] However, it is not Hume but Smith who is most startling in the way that he prefigures current discussion.[2] The opening few pages of his *The Theory of Moral Sentiments* cover many of the arguments found in contemporary work on empathy:

As we have no immediate experience of what other men feel, we can form no idea of the manner in which they are affected, but by conceiving what we ourselves would feel in the like situation. Though our brother is upon the rack, as long as we ourselves are at our ease, our senses will never inform us of what he suffers. They never did, and never can, carry us beyond our own person, and it is by the imagination only that we can form any conception of what are his sensations. Neither can that faculty help us to this any other way, than by representing to us what would be our own, if we were in his case. It is the impressions of our own senses only, not those of his, which our own imaginations copy. By the imagination we place ourselves in his situation, we conceive ourselves enduring all the same torments, we enter as it were into his body, and become in some measure the same person with him, and thence form some idea of his sensations, and even feel something which, though weaker in degree, is not altogether unlike them. (Smith 2002 I.i.i.2)

Neither is it those circumstances only, which create pain and sorrow, that call forth our fellow-feeling. Whatever is the passion which arises from any object in the person principally concerned, an analogous emotion springs up, at the thought of his situation, in the breast of every attentive spectator. (Smith 2002: I.i.i.4)

Hume was concerned with the passions of other people affecting the passions we feel ourselves. Smith's concern is more complex; in his notion of sympathy, we play a more active part. We imagine ourselves in the circumstances of the other person, imagining enduring what they endure. In some sense we identify with that person, and feel, if not exactly what they feel, at least something commensurate with what they feel. It is in this way that we can move 'beyond our own person' and discover what 'our brother' is feeling. As we shall see, this is very close to at least some of the standard modern accounts of empathy.

If we put aside the history of the phenomenon and look to the history of the term itself, we are taken into a series of debates in German psychology and aesthetics in the late nineteenth century. A key term in such debates was *Einfühlung*. This is difficult to translate literally – it is usually rendered as 'feeling into'. A surprising feature of these debates is that those involved were less interested in sharing mental states with, or projecting mental states into, other *people* as much as they were interested in projecting mental states into other (inanimate) *things*. A good deal of stage-setting took place before the emergence of *Einfühlung* as a concept. Inasmuch as it broadly concerned the relation between active mental life and the inanimate world, at least part of that stage-setting is the concern with the relation between subject and object prevalent in German thought since Kant and Hegel. A further landmark in the history of the concept, which surely had an influence on the more concrete developments at the end of the nineteenth century, was Romanticism, in particular, German Romanticism. The Romantic movement of the late eighteenth and early nineteenth centuries was of such a disparate nature (geographically, politically and in almost every other way) that general claims about it will hardly rise above the banal. However, one characteristic was a yearning for unity against the distinctions characteristic of the time, whether subject and object, mind and body, man and world, or reason and the imagination. Finding a way in which our minds can enter into the world promises one way of approaching such a unity.

One manifestation of this, which took Romanticism closer to the modern use of the term 'empathy', occurs in the work of Johann Gottfried von Herder. Herder uses the term *Einfühlung* in his *This Too a Philosophy of History for the Formation of Humanity* (Herder 1774). Herder's most notable contemporary commentator, Michael Forster, has argued that Herder was not talking about psychological projection (which would take his use close to one important aspect of the modern use) but was using the term metaphorically as a way of describing 'an arduous process of historical-philological enquiry'. The cash value of the metaphor has five components, none of which are particularly part of our history. Two of them, however, do take us close to a few elements of at least some of the modern meaning of the term 'empathy': 'in order to interpret a subject's language one must achieve an imaginative reproduction of his perceptual and affective sensations' and 'the interpreter should strive to develop his grasp of linguistic usage, contextual facts, and relevant sensations to the point where this achieves something of the same immediate, automatic character that it has for a text's original audience when they understood the text in light of such things (so that it acquires for him, as it had for them, the phenomenology more of a feeling than a cognition)' (Forster 2002: xvii–xviii). In short, when we read historical texts we should, in the first instance, imagine ourselves occupying the perspective of the producer of the text including imaginatively reproducing his or her mental states, and, in the second instance, we should do the same for the presumed readership of the text. Furthermore, in the second instance, doing so establishes a link to the feelings.

In 'On the Cognition and Sensation of the Soul', Herder describes the process that becomes central for the later writers we will be considering: 'The more a limb signifies what it is supposed to signify, the more beautiful it is; and only inner sympathy, i.e., feeling and transposition of our whole human self into the form that has been explored by touch, is teacher and indicator of beauty' (Herder 1778, quoted in Jahoda 2005: 154). Herder does not use the term *Einfühlung* ('feeling into') here, but rather 'inner sympathy'. This is symptomatic of things to come; although *Einfühlung* emerges as the favoured term, plenty of other terms flourish in the same hedgerow to indicate either the same or some very similar concept.

The first signs of aesthetics taking up the term in a significant way is in the writings of Friedrich Theodor Vischer, Karl Köstlin and Hermann Lotze (Mallgrave and Ikonomou 1994: 20).[3] However, it was in the doctoral dissertation of Vischer's son, Robert, that *Einfühlung* was first given a technical definition. From the welter of Vischer's theorizing, we can identify three claims that, even if they did not originate with Vischer, were brought together under the concept *Einfühlung*. First, he distinguishes between passive processes – bodily reactions to the world that involve no conscious involvement – and more active processes. He characterizes this distinction in several ways, including sensation versus feeling, sensory empathy versus kinaesthetic empathy and seeing versus scanning. Here is one characterization of whatever it is that is on the first side of the divide: 'By sensation I mean the sensory process only and, more particularly, the sensory response to

an observed object' (Vischer 1873: 95). In their discussion
of Vischer's work, Harry Francis Mallgrave and Eleftherios
Ikonomou list, along with *Einfühlung*, various other terms
which characterize the second part of the divide: 'Anfüh-
lung, Ineinsfühlung, Nachfühlung, Zufühlung, and Zusam-
menfühlung' (Mallgrave and Ikonomou 1994: 22). Whatever
the details, all these involve the active involvement of the
mind and imagination. Second, Vischer claims that a large
part of the passive process lies in a similarity between the
outward forms and the inner processes: 'This is not so much
a harmony within an object as a harmony between the object
and the subject, which arises because the object has a harmo-
nious form and the formal effect corresponding to subjective
harmony' (Vischer 1873: 95). Finally, Vischer introduces the
notion of projection. In this, he was influenced by a book
by Karl Albert Scherner, *Das Leben des Traums* (*The Life
of the Dream*), which had been published in 1861 (Scherner
1861). The passage in which Vischer describes this influence,
culminating in his definition of *Einfühlung*, is worth quoting
in full:

> The longer I concerned myself with this concept of a pure
> symbolism of form, the more it seemed to me possible to
> distinguish between ideal associations and a direct merger of
> the imagination with objective form. This latter possibility
> became clear to me with the help of Karl Albert Scherner's
> book *Das Leben des Traums* (The life of the dream). This
> profound work, feverishly probing hidden depths, contains a
> veritable wealth of highly instructive examples that make it
> possible for any reader who finds himself unsympathetic with
> the mystical form of the generally abstract passages to arrive
> at an independent conclusion. Particularly valuable in an aes-
> thetic sense is the section on 'Die symbolische Grundforma-
> tion für die Leibreize' (Symbolic basic formation for bodily
> stimuli). Here it was shown how the body, in responding to
> certain stimuli in dreams, objectifies itself in spatial forms.
> Thus it unconsciously projects its own bodily form – and with
> this also the soul – into the form of the object. From this I
> derived the notion that I call 'empathy' [*Einfühlung*]. (Vischer
> 1873: 92)

There is at least one puzzle here: what Vischer means
when he says that the body 'objectifies itself in spatial forms'.

He approaches, but never clearly says, that we identify ourselves with the object. The simile he uses to make his point – 'we have the wonderful ability to project our own physical form into an objective form in much the same way as wild fowlers gain access to their quarry by concealing themselves in a blind' – is evocative, but hardly perspicuous (Vischer 1873: 100).

In short, in Vischer's work, we see the outline of the contemporary concept of empathy coming together. The three claims distinguished above foreshadow three elements of the contemporary concept. First, his distinction between passive and active processes is in some ways akin to the distinction between (as we would put it) the sub-personal and the personal. Second, he has the notion of a process whereby the inner mental states mirror outer forms. Finally, he has the notion of our projecting selves into an object and in that way imbuing the form of that object with content. However, quite what 'imbuing' covers here is unclear.

If Vischer perhaps deserves to be relegated to being a footnote in this history, the same should not be said of the man who picked up and developed his ideas: Theodor Lipps. Lipps has rather faded into obscurity, but, in his time, he was a major intellectual figure. Had T. E. Hulme[4] lived to complete his planned work on 'Modern Theories of Art', two and a half of the projected nine chapters would have been devoted to Lipps (Hulme 1924: 261–4). This would, no doubt, have led to more of Lipps's work being translated into English, which could have shored up his reputation in anglophone countries. As it is, it is rare to find him mentioned anywhere apart from accounts of the genesis of 'empathy'.

At any particular time Lipps seems to have meant various things by *Einfühlung*, and he also shifted his view so that he meant different things at different times. The principal statement of his view is in his 1903 article, ' "Empathy", Inward Imitation, and Sense Feelings' (Lipps 1903).[5] A contemporary review of his work puts it in a recognizably Vischerean context:

Of late the question, or rather group of questions, which has excited most debate among German aestheticians has to do with the distinction between the object immediately presented to sense-perception – say a rose with its characteristic form and colouring – and the meaning which this has for our imagination, say full vitality and pride of life. (Anonymous 1908: 459)

Lipps distinguishes 'aesthetic' imitation from what he calls 'voluntary' imitation (Lipps 1903: 254). His account of the first is radical. Faced with an aesthetic object, I feel various powerful and active emotions: 'I feel myself strong, light, sure, resilient, perhaps proud and the like'. Furthermore, 'It is myself' that I feel as having these emotions. So far, so good. The radical element is how he gets those felt emotions 'into' the object. He does so by identification: 'I do not so feel myself in relation to the thing or over against it, but in it...This is what I mean by Empathy: that the distinction between the self and the object disappears or rather does not yet exist' (Lipps 1903: 253). Lipps gives various other formulations of a similar sort ('I am even spatially in its position, so far as the self has a spatial position; I am transported into it' (Lipps 1903: 254)), although the idea does not become less obscure. There is some degree of backtracking which at least makes clear that Lipps is not claiming any straightforward identity between the observer and the object:

> In unimitative movement the activity belongs to my real self, my whole personality endowed as it actually is, with all its sensations, ideas, thoughts, feelings, and especially with the motive or inner occasion from which the movement springs. In aesthetic imitation, on the other hand, the self is an ideal self. But this must not be misunderstood. The ideal self too is real, but it is not the practical self. It is the contemplative self which only exists in the lingering contemplation of the object. (Lipps 1903: 255)

In common with other commentators, both those contemporary with Lipps and those writing more recently, I find his account of 'aesthetic empathy' obscure. However, it was the non-aesthetic use Lipps made of the concept that arguably has had the greater effect on contemporary thought. This is a significant step in the history of the concept; the move from empathy with objects to empathy with people.

Lipps moves seamlessly between talk of an object of beauty to talk of broader properties of – specifically – human beings.

His example of something 'strong, proud, and free' is in fact 'a human figure':

> I see a man making powerful, free, light, perhaps courageous
> motions of some kind, which are objects of my full attention.
> I feel a sense of effort. I may carry this out in real imitative
> movements. If so, I feel myself active. I do not merely imagine
> but feel the endeavour, the resistance of obstacles, the over-
> coming, the achievement. (Lipps 1903: 253–4)

In this passage, we have the familiar idea of ourselves undergoing various perturbations, in this case including motor
perturbations, and feel what it is that the person in front of
me is undergoing. We know from work produced by Lipps in
1907 that he put his concept of *Einfühlung* to work in thinking about the so-called 'problem of other minds'. In fact, the
problem of other minds is really two problems: how we can
know that others have minds at all, and how (once we are
content they do have minds) we can know what goes on in
those minds. I shall refer to these as the 'whether' problem
and the 'how' problem. The 'whether' problem arises because,
although each of us is acquainted with our own mind, we
are not acquainted with the minds of others. Without such
acquaintance, what justification do we have for thinking
others have minds? Descartes had posed the problem vividly
in the seventeenth century: 'I chanced, however, to look out
of the window, and see men walking in the street; now I
say in ordinary language that I "see" them...but what can
I "see" besides hats and coats, which may cover automata?'
(Descartes 1970: 73). A venerable solution to the 'whether'
problem is 'the argument from analogy'. I know, in my own
case, that certain mental states come between certain inputs
and certain outputs. For example, I know that between the
input of my hitting my thumb with a hammer and the output
of my crying out there is the sensation of pain. Other people
are similar to me in all kinds of ways, so I infer that, between
similar inputs and similar outputs, other people have mental
states similar to the ones with which I am acquainted in
my own case. An almost equally venerable rebuttal of this
argument is that it is methodologically suspect. As I am
only acquainted with a single case (my own), it would be

irresponsible for me to make an inference regarding how other people feel; there are no grounds for thinking others are like me in this respect (Ryle 1963: 52).

Lipps, rightly unconvinced by the argument from analogy, sought to replace it with an 'instinct' which gives us knowledge of other minds without involving an inference:[6]

> In the perception and comprehension of certain sensory objects, namely, those that we afterward represent as the body of another individual (or generally as the sensory appearance of such), is immediately grasped by us. This applies particularly to the perception and comprehension of occurrences or changes in this sensory appearance, which we name, for example, friendliness or sadness. This grasp happens immediately and simultaneously with the perception, and that does not mean that we see it or apprehend it by means of the senses. We cannot do that, since anger, friendliness, or sadness cannot be perceived through the senses. We can only experience this kind of thing in ourselves. (Lipps 1907: 713; quoted in Jahoda 2005: 156; translated by Jahoda)

Lipps proposed that our grasp of other minds is a result of two processes. In the words of Gustave Jahoda, 'the object of sensory perception comes from the external world, while the inner excitation comes from within ourselves' (Jahoda 2005: 156). I witness another person's gesture of, for example, anger, and this raises a feeling within my consciousness. It is unclear how this could be a solution to the problem of whether other people have minds – we would simply be acquainted with more of our own mental states. However, if we put the 'whether' problem to one side (or assume it is solved), we do look to have a solution to the 'how' problem. We manage to 'read' the minds of others by re-experiencing their mental states for ourselves.

This leads naturally to the term's original introduction into English (at least as 'empathy' – in 1908 the term had been translated as 'infeeling' (Anonymous 1908: 466)). Here is the passage in which the psychologist Edward Titchener coined the term:

> Not only do I see gravity and modesty and pride and courtesy and stateliness, but I feel or act them in the mind's muscles.

This is, I suppose, a simple case of empathy, if we may coin that term as a rendering of *Einfühlung*; there is nothing curious or idiosyncratic about it; but it is a fact that must be mentioned. (Titchener 1909: 21–2; quoted in Jahoda 2005: 161)

'The mind's muscles' is an inspired description. In the same way as a frustrated football manager finds himself exercising his leg muscles by mimicking on the sidelines his players' kicks in the field, so our minds' muscles mimic in our minds what is going on in the minds of others. The non-aesthetic developments of Lipps's thoughts, the empathy with people and the subsequent broadening into the notion of other minds, are what take us closer to the modern conceptions of empathy.

The schema for ascertaining what is going on in the minds of others is perfectly general. There is no reason to limit it to finding out what emotion a person is feeling; it looks as if it could be anything that is going on in the mind of another (I will be drawing various limits to this claim throughout the book). This is in tension with the common view of empathy (such as it is) that links it particularly to *emotional* states. Indeed, we have already seen that empathy is an unholy amalgam of a raft of different claims involving imagining another's perspective, mirroring the properties of others (whether things or people), projecting our mental states into others (whether things or people) and taking on the emotions of others. This terrible tangle of issues, as we shall see, continues to dog the contemporary discussion.

Indeed, this terrible tangle puts an obstacle in the way of fulfilling the laudable aim of books in this series: namely, to give a synoptic view of some key concept. This presupposes that there is some unity to the concept of which a synoptic view could be taken. Perhaps matters are not quite as bad as I am making them out to be; Heidi Maibom, in her introduction to a recent collection of essays on the topic, claims that 'the rumors about the impossibly diverse usage of "empathy" are exaggerated' (Maibom 2014: 2). However, the characterization she goes on to give (quoted above), in its focus on empathetic emotions and on caring behaviour leading from such emotions, only covers a proportion of what is discussed, currently, under the term 'empathy'. In particular, it ignores the discussions focusing on epistemology which do not take there to be a link between empathy and the emotions, and which are far removed from particular sorts of behaviour. I side with Dominic McIver Lopes who writes that 'Experts characterize what they call "empathy" in several incompatible ways, and perhaps the definitions glom onto distinct phenomena, none of which has the sole claim to the title of "empathy"' (Lopes 2011: 121).[7]

Coming to terms with the difficulties posed by the fact that there are many different phenomena, all of which lay claim to the term, has dictated the shape of this book; I have largely restricted myself to Anglo-American philosophy, broadly construed. This does not mean that issues such as, for example, the nature of explanation in the human sciences have been ignored; it means, rather, that the focus has been on philosophy written in English. However, even with such a restriction, the scope of the book is fairly vast. Chapters 3 and 4 focus on the philosophy of mind, in which the concept of empathy has been central to one of the recent Homeric struggles concerning interpersonal understanding (I shall use the term 'interpersonal understanding', although there are other terms in common use such as 'mindreading' (Nichols and Stich 2003: 1)). Chapter 3 will motivate the claim that empathy, or 'simulation', is a key component of interpersonal understanding and then focus on the deliberate efforts we might make to work out what is going on in someone else's head and to predict their behaviour. Chapter 4 will then try to map the various attempts to argue for simulation. First, I will discuss whether we can come to see that we are committed to there being some degree of empathy (or 'simulation' or 'co-cognition') simply by reflecting on what we know about how we understand each other. This contrasts with the discussion in the second half of the chapter, which has an empirical focus; that the claim that there is some degree of empathy in our interpersonal understanding is a hypothesis that needs to be tested against rival hypotheses. In particular, it will look at the work of Alvin Goldman, and then at contemporary work on 'mirror neurons' before a brief look at the approach known as 'homuncular functionalism'. Chapter 5 continues to investigate attempts to use something like empathy to understand what goes on in the heads of others. However, in this case it concerns what it is to have a full grasp of others' reasons for action. This evaluates a set of arguments from R. G. Collingwood about the nature of historical explanation; arguments which have recently been revised and reasserted by Karsten Stueber. Chapter 6 changes the focus from broad epistemic questions to what is perhaps a more familiar discussion in non-philosophical circles: empathizing with someone with respect to the emotions they are feeling. This leads, in chapter 7, to a discussion of the role that empathy plays in our moral lives – or indeed of whether it plays a role at all. What is revealed is a schism between the popular view of empathy as being an unequivocal moral good, and the dominant view in both psychology and philosophy, which is more ambivalent. Chapter 8 takes us back to the origins of the concept in aesthetics. We will see that empathy had a limited role in early twentieth-century theorizing but has had a return, particularly in the philosophy of literature. The final chapter attempts some summary, and speculates about the future of the concept. This includes a look at a recent attempt to remove empathy from our picture of interpersonal understanding and to take a broader, more social approach.

Given the truth of Lopes's observation, this book is more of a smorgasbord than an overview. That such an approach is necessary is part of the interest of the current debate. Although there is some overlap, and accumulation of argument, I have written it in such a way that I hope the chapters can be read independently. There are, however, some distinctions common to several of the discussions that need to be drawn, which will be the subject of the next chapter.

2

Some Conceptual
Preliminaries

In the last chapter I gave a rough characterization of empathy as *using our imaginations as a tool so as to adopt a different perspective in order to grasp how things appear (or feel) from there*. One manifestation of this, which plays a prominent role in current debates, is simulation:[1] we use our own minds as a model of other minds. I shall introduce the idea by borrowing an analogy from Jane Heal:

> We can get at the key idea by considering the familiar example of the model aircraft in the wind tunnel. (The case has some misleading features, which we shall need to remark later, but it will serve to get us started.) Suppose that we know, in general terms, that aerofoils provide lift, that aircraft are liable to become unstable in some circumstances and the like, but lack any detailed quantitative theory of aerodynamics. We do not have a set of usable equations relating all the significant variables, such as body shape or wind speed, to the upshots, such as lift and stability, in which we are interested. How can it be that we may nevertheless arrive at detailed quantitative predictions on these matters? Here is a possible method. If we are convinced (for example, by inductive generalisation, or as a consequence of theoretical assumptions) that a model aircraft will behave similarly to a real aircraft of the same shape, at least in a usefully wide range of circumstances, then we may test models with varying shape in varying wind speeds and so on, measuring the quantitative outcome in various

respects and using those figures as a basis for the needed detailed predictions of the actual aircraft. We use the model aircraft to simulate the real aircraft. (Heal 1996a: 64–5)[2]

As Heal points out, we could learn something only if the 'model aircraft will behave similarly to a real aircraft of the same shape'. Analogously, simulation will only work if the model (our mind) behaves similarly to that of which it is a model (I shall refer to the person to whom our attention is directed as 'the target'). If we assume our mental machinery and that of the target are roughly the same then all we need to do is find some way of replicating *their* inputs into *our* machinery, and this should yield an output from *our* machinery which is the same as the output from *their* machinery. Whether or not differences between us render empathy epistemically unreliable is, as we shall see, a matter for considerable dispute. There is also an issue of what can be simulated. Wind tunnels can test for certain properties of aircraft, but they will not answer all of an engineer's questions. Analogously, the scope of empathy – that is, which kinds of mental states can be simulated – is also open to dispute.

In addition to worries about the reliability and scope of simulation, two further issues arise. First, there are differences in the means by which we marshal the resources needed to take on the perspective of the target. The simplest case might be that in which we are in direct perceptual contact with the target. For example, you might be watching someone out of the window about to get into his car. As he does so, without realizing it, he drops his keys. You could simulate being in his situation; you 'input' that you put your hand in your pocket and find nothing there. Your simulation yields the thought that you would check all your other pockets, before looking on the ground around you. Having noted these 'outputs' in your own case, you attribute them to the target. This is, in fact, what the target does; your simulation has been successful. In cases in which you are in direct perceptual contact with the target, you do not need to exercise your imagination; all you need to do is to think what they are thinking. As we shall see, some count this as an exercise of the imagination (after all, the input is not the belief that *you* have lost *your* keys). In addition to direct perceptual contact, there are various other means by which you could marshal the resources you need. Someone could describe a set of events from the perspective of the target. You would not need to imagine (in the sense of 'make up') the circumstances; you are being told them. However, it might require an exercise of the imagination to adopt the target's point of view; to come up with the right inputs from what you have been told. Finally, we might simply imagine a set of circumstances from the perspective of someone in those circumstances; it might be some actual person, some hypothetical person, or some type of person (such as a Roman soldier who trudged along this road (Goldie 2000: 204)). This might require some effort; you might need to imaginatively engage your senses and engage in visualizing or imagining sounds. Indeed, as we shall see, the effort required arguably renders the process epistemically unreliable.

The second issue concerns the nature of the inputs. As it is a simulation, the inputs are not true of the simulator. That is, when I simulate the person who has dropped his keys, the input is not 'He has dropped his keys' but 'I have dropped my keys'. What is important is that these simulacra of beliefs ('make-beliefs', as they have come to be called) turn the simulator's cognitive machinery in the same way that beliefs turn the target's cognitive machinery. The output (check the other pockets, look on the ground) stop short of action by the simulator; you do not check your pockets, or look on the ground around where you are sitting. Rather, the output is some kind of representation of the motivation to so act; which motivation you then attribute to the target. Empathy, construed as simulation, needs it to be the case that make-beliefs have a similar enough effect on the simulator's mental machinery as do beliefs on the target's mental machinery. If not, the output from the simulator's mental machinery will not be a reliable guide as to the target's mental state. As we shall see, this too is open to dispute. We should note, as it has caused some confusion, that generally we regard the make-belief states as tracking the truth about the world, even if they are not true of us but true of someone else. We make-believe that there is nothing in our pockets because we believe that the target believes there is nothing in their pockets. That is, the distinction here between make-beliefs and beliefs is not the distinction between stuff we make up and stuff we do not make up, or fiction and non-fiction.

The characterization of empathy as simulation, which has the broad purpose of finding out what is going on in someone else's head, whatever that might be, is more characteristic of academic philosophy than it is of discussions outside that discipline. Outside academic philosophy there is more of a focus on affective or emotional states (which I shall call 'narrow empathy'). That is, to empathize with someone is not to imagine the world from their perspective so as to discover what they are thinking or what they will do next, but to imagine the world from their perspective so as to feel what they feel. For those for whom 'empathy' means 'narrow empathy', there is an essential link with the emotions. Those who do think thus might wonder why three entire chapters of this book are taken up with something that seems to lack this essential link. My defence of this is twofold. First, we should not take it for granted that academic philosophy is the outlier. In the most in-depth monograph on empathy to date, Karsten Stueber claims that it is the philosophers who have grasped the interesting core of the concept (a claim supported by the brief history of the concept given in the last chapter):

> I would object to the claim that empathy as a vicarious sharing of an emotional state should be understood as the only right way of defining and explicating the concept of empathy, as it is sometimes asserted in this context. Empathy as understood within the original philosophical context is best seen as a form of *inner or mental imitation for the purpose of gaining knowledge of other minds.* (Stueber 2006: 28; emphasis in original)

The second consideration is that empathy as a broad epistemic concept, and empathy as a narrow affective concept, share a common core: they both centrally involve taking on the perspective of the other. Although the philosophical account has come to be known as 'simulation theory', a name that seems to take it away from our concerns here, it is altogether possible that it might instead have been known as 'the empathy view' (see Davies and Stone 1995: 1; and Goldman 2006: 17). Furthermore, there are several wrinkles in sorting out a defensible version of the broad notion of empathy, which carry over to sorting out a defensible version of narrow empathy.

Narrow empathy comes in two forms. First, the link with the emotions might simply be that we imagine being in someone's circumstances so as to find out what they are feeling. We can consider the kind of example that Barack Obama had in mind in his talk of 'the empathy deficit'. We make the effort to take on the perspective of someone who has been made redundant. We simulate all kinds of input: worry about the effect on his or her family, worry about paying the mortgage, belief that people with his or her set of skills face limited opportunities and so on. We find ourselves experiencing something like a feeling of panic. Hence, we attribute to him or her a feeling of panic. (We shall see, in the next chapter, that such examples are controversial.) In such cases, the essential link with the emotions is simply that simulation does not count as empathy unless our imaginative endeavours have, as their output, an emotional state. However, using our imaginations to learn what the target is experiencing is not the only, or even the usual form of narrow empathy. The term more usually describes a situation in which one believes that the target is experiencing some emotion, and one takes on his or her perspective, not to learn what emotion he or she is experiencing, but simply to show fellow-feeling, or solidarity, by sharing that emotion (or something like it). Joel Smith has termed this 'transparent fellow feeling' (Smith 2015).

One might describe this contrast as being between empathy functioning epistemically (finding out how the target feels) and it functioning for reasons of solidarity (simply sharing the target's emotion). Smith sees matters differently. He argues that the latter, which is what he takes empathy to be, is itself functioning epistemically. He argues that unless we have transparent fellow-feeling, there is some knowledge we lack about the target's emotional state. We can know *what* they feel (panic), but we do not know *how* they feel: 'I suggest that A knows how B feels only if she knows that B is Ψ and how it feels to be Ψ. Further, A knows how it feels to be Ψ if and only if A knows that Ψ feels like *this*' (Smith 2015: 5). It is the second of Smith's two claims that is controversial. Why should we think that A only knows how it feels to be Ψ, if A can occurrently identify Ψ in her own case? However, the claim is less strong than it might appear. Smith allows that to be in a position to judge that 'Ψ feels like *this*', all A needs is to have some version of something like the state (which might come about as a result of simulation, calling up the state from episodic memory, or perhaps by some other means). In other words, provided A is familiar with Ψ, it will be difficult for her to bring it to mind without also bringing to mind some token of it to which she can refer. Independently, Kendall Walton has worked out a similar account. His (characteristically revisionary) account takes the core notion of 'empathy' to be someone using their mental state as a sample for the mental state of another: we take the other to be feeling like *this*, where 'this' refers to our own mental state (Walton 2015: 5–10).

I shall not take a stand on Smith's contention that transparent fellow-feeling fills in what would otherwise be a gap in our knowledge of the target's emotion; that is, whether it is impossible to know how the target is feeling unless one knows that the target feels like *this*, where 'this' refers to one's own occurrent mental state. I will also not discuss Kendall Walton's suggestion, which is too revisionary to belong to a book of this sort (although it does get a brief mention again in chapter 6). I shall, however, make use of Smith's characterization of transparent fellow-feeling. Sometimes our motivation for empathizing with another is nothing to do with discovering what is going on in their heads, but sharing what is in their heads. As Smith notes, the point had been made many years ago by his namesake, Adam Smith: 'nothing pleases us more than to observe in other men a fellow-feeling with all the emotions of our own breast' (Smith 2002: I.i.ii.1).[3]

So far, I have been speaking of empathy as something that happens above the level of consciousness. However, some philosophers, notably those closer to the cognitive sciences, extend the term to sub-personal systems by which we come to understand each other (here we have to construe 'understand' broadly enough so as to cover the sub-personal). We met a paradigm instance of this in the last chapter, in the quotation from Hume. This was an instance of the phenomenon of 'emotional contagion': 'As in strings equally wound up, the motion of one communicates itself to the rest; so all the affections readily pass from one person to the other, and beget correspondent movements in every human creature.' This is a fairly familiar experience; anxious people tend to make people around them anxious; we can 'catch' the joy from a crowd of joyful people. Stephen Davies has given a more formal analysis:

> Emotional contagion involves the arousal in B by A of an affect that corresponds either to an affect felt and displayed by A or, where A is non-sentient, as for the case of music and house décors, to the expressive character experienced by B as displayed in A's appearance, and while B's arousal must derive from A's displaying the relevant affect, so that A's affect is the perceptual object of B's reaction, A's affect is not the emotional object of B's response, because B does not believe (or imagine) of A's affect what is required to make it an appropriate emotional object of the response B experiences. (Davies 2011: 146)

It is not required, for something to count as an instance of emotional contagion, that the person affected is aware of the cause of their affect, or even consciously aware that they have been affected. The mechanisms of contagion are distinctly sub-personal – here described by Amy Coplan:

> The main processes involved in contagion are motor mimicry and the activation and the feedback it generates. Initiated by direct sensory perception, these processes do not involve the imagination, nor are they based on any cognitive evaluation or complex appraisal. Thus emotional contagion is a bottom-up process that operates much like a form of perception. We encounter another person, automatically react to the other's expressions of emotion through involuntary imitation, and end up experiencing the same emotion ourselves. (Coplan 2011: 8)

These mechanisms are not only sub-personal; they do not involve any kind of perspective-taking (we shall find, later in the book, arguments for there being sub-personal instances of perspective taking). In short, emotional contagion does not seem to fall under even the rough, and deliberately wide, working definition of 'empathy' I gave earlier. This suggests that conceptual hygiene is served by distinguishing emotional contagion from empathy, reserving the latter for activities that involve taking the perspective of the other (which is, indeed, the line Coplan takes (Coplan 2011: 9)).

Coplan is surely right to want to mark this distinction, but I shall not take a strong line on the use of the term. To do so would be to cause a twofold problem. First, it would make it difficult to discuss the views of those in the area who do count emotional contagion as a form of empathy (Maibom 2014: 4). Second, and relatedly, the kinds of mirroring mechanisms that underpin emotional contagion underpin capacities that are broader and more significant. Alvin Goldman has argued that such automatic mechanisms play an important role in interpersonal understanding; these he describes as 'low level empathy' (Goldman 2006). Karsten Stueber uses the term 'basic empathy' to refer to 'mechanisms that underlie our theoretically unmediated quasi-perceptual ability to recognize other creatures directly as minded creatures and to recognize them implicitly as creatures that are fundamentally like us' (Stueber 2006: 20).

A distinction I shall observe, however, is that between empathy and sympathy. We have seen that Hume and Smith used the term 'sympathy' to cover a range of phenomena, including the kind of perspective-taking we now associate with empathy. In current debates, a broad consensus has emerged to use the terms to distinguish between two different phenomena (or, rather, the collection of phenomena that go by the name 'empathy' and some other, more clearly defined, phenomenon that goes by the name 'sympathy'). The standard case of sympathy is that in which the target feels some negative emotion, to which the person feeling sympathy feels, well, sympathetic (I have described this as 'the standard case' as there are others as well). Some want to extend the term to cover cases in which a target is feeling a positive emotion, and so that we can 'sympathize' with the success of others (Maibom 2014: 3). I am sure that some people do use the term in this way, but I shall put this use aside in my discussion as the case of sympathizing with another's unhappiness is more central. We speak of someone who has suffered a chance misfortune as 'deserving of sympathy'; we would not usually say that of someone who had won the lottery.

What is it to 'feel sympathetic'? In the standard case, a person comes to believe that the target is in some kind of distress; that is, they are in pain, or they are feeling one of the negative emotions. Such a person might come to this belief by perception (they can see that the target is in distress) or via testimony (they are reliably informed that the target is in distress). This provokes in them a feeling which is directed towards the target. We are not generally very precise in the way we describe this feeling. We sometimes simply describe it as 'sympathy'; we claim to feel 'a great deal of sympathy for so-and-so'. Sometimes we might describe it as 'pity', 'concern', 'sadness', 'compassion' or simply 'feeling sorry for'.

There are two important contrasts with empathy. First, sympathy does not necessarily involve imagining what it is like for the other person. All that is needed is that the person comes to believe that the target is distressed and, as I said above, they can come to this belief in a variety of ways. Second, sympathy does not necessarily involve having the same feeling as the other person. That is, it is not part of the phenomenon that we feel exactly what they feel. Rather, we are feeling an emotion (sympathy) towards them. Indeed, to move from the 'standard' case described above, it is possible to feel sympathy towards someone who is not themselves feeling an emotion. Someone could be in a terrible situation but, because of their resolute Stoicism or because of a brain injury, they do not feel distress. They would still be a proper target for sympathy.

It is not part of my claim that all phenomena can be neatly classified under one of the headings given above. Consider seeing someone shut their fingers in a car door. The car door shuts, they cry out with pain, and you, the witness, wince horribly. Is this sympathy, empathy, emotional contagion or something else? It does not seem quite like sympathy; what we feel is something like pain, rather than any feeling of sympathy (although, of course, a feeling of sympathy might quickly follow). Is it then empathy – albeit a very simple form of empathy? No, for two reasons. First, we do not imagine what it is like to be the person. At least, we do not consciously imagine this; although there might be some measure of automatic perspective-taking (I say more about this below). Second, we do not have the same feeling as the target; we do not feel pain. It is true that there is an overlap between the areas of the brain that are active when we witness pain and the areas of the brain that are active when we feel pain ourselves (Maibom 2014: 9). However, this is not enough to say that the witness feels pain; we do not feel what the person who shut their fingers in the door feels, even to a degree. For the same reason it is not an instance of emotional contagion; pain is not the kind of sensation that can be spread in this way. It does not fit neatly under any of these headings but partakes of a little of each of them. To conclude, that is not a problem – there is no reason to think that all mental phenomena can be neatly divided so as to fit into a number of headings specified in advance.

3
Empathy as Simulation

As discussed in chapter 2, outside philosophy empathy has been largely associated with taking the perspective of another so as to share their emotions, or, at least, to get a better appreciation of their concerns. Within philosophy most of the debate has been in a quite different area: that of interpersonal understanding. In order to see where empathy comes in, I shall need to put in place some of the other pieces of the debate; in particular, the account which the 'empathy theory' sought to replace.

Let us begin with a very broad question. How is it that we understand things? That is, how is it that the world does not usually surprise us? When I press the 'on' switch on my radio it comes on (all things being equal). When I push the pedal down on my bicycle, the back wheel goes round (all things being equal). There does not seem any great mystery here. I have learned, either from experience or by working it out, that when I press the 'on' switch the radio comes on and when I press the pedal the back wheel goes round. I have beliefs of the following sort: in circumstances C, if P happens then Q will happen (all things being equal). We need the 'all things being equal' clause because, occasionally, P will happen and Q not happen. These will be the occasions when, perhaps, the batteries in the radio have run out of power, or the chain has fallen off the bicycle. To introduce a bit of jargon, we might say that we have (rather elementary) *theories* as to how radios work and how bicycles work.

Does this general account of the way we understand things cover the way we understand people? One might think that it does. After all, it is plausible that people are only rather complicated machines. The general schema I gave in the previous paragraph might seem to apply. In the usual circumstances, if people want X, and they believe that doing Y will bring them X, and there is nothing else to be said against doing Y, then they will do Y. If Jane would like coffee, and she believes going to the café will enable her to buy coffee, and she has time to go to the café and the means to buy coffee, then I shall not be surprised if she goes to the café. Each of us is aware of a vast body of information about the causes and effects of psychological states. We may well be consciously aware of part of this body of information, but the greater part of it we know implicitly. It could not be that we employ it consciously; that would be far too laborious, and our interactions with other people and the world generally would grind to a halt. However, the way we understand other people is by applying this information to what we know about the particular person in front of us so as to come up with a prediction about what is going on in their heads or about their subsequent behaviour. This account of how we understand each other is known as 'theory theory': that is, it is the *theory* that we each have a *theory* as to how people work.

Theory theory is part of a larger view of the mind and mental states known as functionalism; the view that mental states are identified with 'functional roles', rather than states of the soul or states of the brain. A mental state's functional role is given in terms of its characteristic inputs, outputs and relations to other mental states. Hence, the role can be captured by the kinds of information embodied in the theory described above (whether those are laws, some other kinds of nomological generalization, or mere rules of thumb). In recent years, functionalism has been the dominant account of the mind, and, as a result, theory theory has been the dominant account of interpersonal understanding. The reaction against theory theory began in 1986 when two philosophers independently proposed an alternative; in the United States, Robert M. Gordon wrote 'Folk Psychology as Simulation' and, in the United Kingdom, Jane Heal wrote 'Replication and Functionalism' (Gordon 1986; Heal 1986). This alternative proposal holds that we do not bring theoretical knowledge to bear in understanding each other, but rather we simulate: we imagine ourselves in the position of the other. There were differences both of substance and emphasis in Gordon's and Heal's accounts, and, since then, the literature has blossomed and brought forth many further accounts.

The principal argument against theory theory is its basic implausibility. It would be a dizzying task to articulate the theory that we would need to understand other people. The elements of the theory would be people's mental states: beliefs, desires, hopes, fears and so on. The theory would need to relate those elements in the kind of schema we saw above: 'When someone is in so-and-so combination of mental states and receives sensory stimuli of so-and-so kind, he tends with so-and-so probability to be caused thereby to go into so-and-so mental states and produce so-and-so motor responses' (Lewis 1972: 272). Here are two reasons why attributing such a theory to each of us is implausible. First, it is not clear what it means to say that each of us *possesses* such a theory. Second, it is not clear that there could actually be any such theory; that is, it is not clear that such a theory could be formulated, even in principle.

How could we show that we possess and use such a theory? We might think we could borrow a thought from the less sophisticated end of theories of artificial intelligence. The thought is that if we build a machine that can do everything we can do (that, at a minimum, could pass 'the Turing test'), then we have created something akin to ourselves in respect of how our minds work. That is, a machine that has the same capacities as us must, with respect to those capacities, work in the same way as we do. Let us assume that we could specify the enormously complicated theory that would be needed. Let us further assume that we could, even if only in principle, build a machine that, using such a theory, is able to interact with other people in a way that mimics how we actually do interact with other people. According to the above thought, this would be enough to show that we actually use such a theory. However, would building a machine that mimicked our behaviour by using a theory show that we actually possess and make use of that theory? It would not; it is simply a mistake to think that if we build a machine that does what we do, that shows that we work in the way in which the machine works (see Blackburn 1995: 275). Theory theory also needs to show that we indeed possess and use such a theory.

The demand that theory theory show that we possess and use a theory sets (perhaps) an impossibly high benchmark for success. An alternative that some theory theorists have proposed is to show that their claims conform to 'the dominant explanatory strategy' in cognitive science. The case has been made by Stephen Stitch and Shaun Nichols:

> [T]he dominant explanatory strategy proceeds by positing an internally represented 'knowledge structure' – typically a body of rules or principles or propositions – which serves to guide the execution of the capacity to be explained. These rules or principles or propositions are often described as the agent's 'theory' of the domain in question. In some cases, the theory may be partly accessible to consciousness; the agent can tell us some of the rules or principles he is using. More often, however, the agent has no conscious access to the knowledge guiding his behavior. The theory is 'tacit' or 'sub-doxastic'. (Stich and Nichols 1992: 123)

According to Stitch and Nichols, this strategy has been used successfully in explaining the acquisition, production and comprehension of natural language; the ability to solve mathematical problems; the ability to recognize, manipulate and predict the behaviour of physical objects; and 'a host' of other problems. They cite, in support, many of the leading researchers in cognitive science.

Of course, this does not prove we do possess a tacit psychological theory; there are several areas of doubt. It might be that, for all its explanatory success, the 'dominant explanatory strategy' is incorrect; it might be that it is correct, but that there are disanalogies between our mastery of (for example) natural language and our mastery of folk psychology; and it might be that our mastery of folk psychology cannot be given theoretical form. However, Stich and Nichols have at least given us reason to doubt the initial charge that we cannot possess and use a tacit psychological theory.

In addition to pointing to the difficulties with theory theory, simulation theory has some positive arguments as to why we should accept it. Consider first an everyday situation. You are at work when someone knocks on your office door and returns your car keys that you had dropped earlier. Once the gratitude has subsided, you wonder what you would have done had your keys been lost. That is, you wonder what you would have done were the world different. On the theory-theory scenario you would employ your tacit theoretical knowledge: in circumstances C, were I to believe X and desire Y, then (all things being equal) I would do Z. That, however, does not seem plausible. What seems more plausible is that you would imagine that you had lost your keys and then deliberate; reason and reflect to see what feelings, decisions and actions would emerge. The extension to simulation theory is obvious. If this is what we do when grasping at what *we* would think were we occupying some situation that we are not currently occupying, then we can use the same capacities and methods to grasp what *others* would think were they occupying some situation that we are not currently occupying. In both cases we are thinking of the world from some other perspective; in the first case the perspective of ourselves (albeit not our actual selves as we have not actually lost our keys) and in the second case the perspective of someone other than ourselves. If we do not use tacit theory in the first case, there is no reason to think we use tacit theory in the second.

A second argument for simulation theory begins by looking at the 'all things being equal' clause in the case of understanding the natural world. I claimed that, to get around the natural world, we need to have beliefs of the following sort: in circumstances C, if P happens then Q will happen (all things being equal). The 'all things being equal' clause is necessary because something could intervene, or be absent, such that P happens and Q does not happen. However, you might think that we could specify C in such a detailed way that the 'all things being equal' clause is redundant. For example, in circumstances C, if I switch on my radio, then the radio will come on. We could specify C as follows: that there is a signal, that the radio can pick up the signal, that the radio's internal workings are all in order and that the radio is connected to a power source. The 'all things being equal' clause is a promissory note; it promises that the circumstances can be spelled out in such a way that what we predict will happen actually will happen.

The argument for simulation theory is that, for psychological laws, the 'all things being equal' clause cannot be dispensed with in this manner (Heal 1996b: 50–9). The promissory note cannot be redeemed, and thus the theory cannot be formulated. The core thought here is famously associated with Donald Davidson:

> We know too much about thought and behaviour to trust exact and universal statements linking them. Beliefs and desires issue in behaviour only as modified and mediated by further beliefs and desires, attitudes and attendings, without limit. (Davidson 1970: 217)

It is the 'without limit' part that is important. Consider an instance of coming to a decision (the example is from Jane Heal). Imagine a doctor who needs to decide whether a patient has measles. One might attempt to specify the beliefs that the doctor needs in order to make the decision: beliefs about the symptoms of measles and about the patient's results when subjected to the standard diagnostic test for measles. That looks enough; why would Davidson say there is 'no limit' on the beliefs the doctor might need in order to make the decision? The reason is that we all have innumerably many beliefs, any one of which is potentially relevant. Heal spells out the way that an apparently unconnected belief we have (that Henry VII was a Tudor) becomes relevant:

> I may already be aware of a few off cases (hitherto ignored or shrugged off as failures of apparatus) which suggest that we are perhaps wrong in thinking the standard diagnostic test conclusive. But when we focus on these cases they hint at the idea that in people of a certain genetic constitution the disease runs a non-standard course in which the test is unreliable. The genetic constitution is common in Wales, and in particular in the Tudor family. And perhaps my patient has boasted of his royal ancestor, Henry VII. Given all this, the information that Henry VII was a Tudor is the crucial fact which links the odd case of my current patient to the other odd cases. The discovery of that link might be the final piece of the jigsaw which stimulates me to reassess the previously accepted view of the

reliability of the test. And, having done so, I then judge that the patient does indeed have the disease, despite the negative result. (Heal 1996b: 52)

There is no theory that can tell us which of our vast web of beliefs might bear on our thoughts. That is, there is no theory of relevance. However, we have the remarkable ability to follow a train of thought and judge 'from the inside' whether or not a thought is relevant. The argument for simulation theory is that we can follow the thought processes of others. When you read Heal's example, you are able to follow the doctor's train of thought. Taking his or her perspective, you can see quite easily how one thought leads to another. As we do not possess a theory of relevance, there is no theory which we grasp implicitly and which we could be using. Rather, we imagine ourselves into the perspective of others and see things 'from the inside' (except this time, of course, it is *their* 'inside'). We use the same ability as we use to spot which of our innumerable beliefs are relevant, to spot which of their beliefs are relevant.

The debate between theory theory and simulation theory has run on for decades, with many twists and turns, and sophisticated attempts to demonstrate the truth of one side rather than the other. It would be impossible to describe all these here (although I shall be considering some additional arguments for simulation theory in the next chapter). I hope, in the above, to at least have introduced the problem and shown why some philosophers have proposed simulation as a favoured alternative.

That there is a debate as to how we achieve interpersonal understanding suggests that we are not conscious of the mechanisms through which we achieve such understanding. If we were conscious of the mechanisms, then the nature of interpersonal understanding would be transparent to us and we would not need to discuss it. There is something to this thought, but we should not accept it uncritically. There are certainly some candidates for simulation – I am thinking of basic 'mirroring responses' – which are below the level of consciousness and, I will argue, cannot be anything but. I consider these in the next chapter. There are, however, a range of cases. In addition to the cases that are merely automatic and to which we have no conscious access, there are cases of interpersonal understanding where we are conscious of something going on, but where the nature of what is going on is not fully transparent to us. That is, even if we are consciously attempting to understand someone else, it may not be transparent to us whether we are employing a tacit theory or simulating. In addition, there are cases in which we consciously set out to empathize with another, fully aware of what we are doing.

Whatever example I take, it will have properties that some theorists will find central and other theorists will find peripheral or problematic. However, we need to start somewhere so I will begin with an example from Robert Gordon. 'You and a friend are hiking up a mountain trail, talking. Suddenly, in mid-sentence, your friend stops in his tracks, blurts out "Go back!" then turns and walks quietly back along the trail' (Gordon 1992: 102). As I said above, we try to get ourselves into a position where the world (including other people) does not surprise us. We are surprised by the actions of our friend. As a result, what we do is to scan the environment for menacing or threatening things. That is, we try to see what our friend saw which prompted him to act the way he did. When we see, further up the track, a grizzly bear, we are no longer surprised by his actions.

In this case, it seems a bit of an over-description to say that you 'imagine yourself into your friend's perspective', or even to describe it as an instance of simulation. You and your friend are in the same position (in that you are standing next to each other) and can be assumed to have the same beliefs and desires with respect to grizzly bears (that they are dangerous and best avoided). Nonetheless, however minimally, you are working out what is going on in your friend's head by imagining how things look from his point of view. There is one sense, however, in which this case differs from simulation as I have characterized it. So far, I have described cases in which one simulates being in the target's circumstances, comes up with an appropriate set of inputs, the wheels of one's mental machinery turn, and one comes up with an output which one attributes to the target. In this case, one has the output (your friend says 'Go back!'); what one needs to work out is the input that produced that output.

An attributor's main items of evidence for many target states are causal effects of those states, so the attributor's mind must proceed from known effects to sought-after causes. First-person verbal reports are one type of example. The attributor works backward from the target's verbal utterance to a prior mental state. Similarly, when an attribution is based on non-verbal behavior, the attributor makes a retrodictive or explanatory transition from the behavior to a preceding state. (Goldman 2006: 183–4)

The process of simulation, as I have so far described it, would not help here. The model I have given is that we input into our minds some analogue of what is going on in the target's mind, we run our mental machinery, see what emerges, and attribute that to the target. In this case we have the target's output; what we need is the input. Unless we are able to run our mental processes backwards, simulation does not seem to be the mechanism with which we operate. However, such a conclusion would be too hasty. What we need is what Alvin Goldman calls the 'generate and test' strategy:

The 'generate' stage produces hypothesized states or state combinations that might be responsible for the observed (or inferred) evidence. Hypothesis generation is presumably executed by nonsimulative methods. The 'test' stage consists of *trying out* one or more of the hypothesized state combinations to see if it would yield the observed evidence. This stage might well employ simulation. One [imagines] being in the hypothesized combination of states, lets an appropriate mechanism operate on them, and sees whether the generated upshot matches the observed upshot. (Goldman 2006: 183–4)

In short, you observe your friend's behaviour and hear him say 'Go back!' You wonder to yourself what the input could have been that had such an output. You scan the world from your friend's perspective (which may well, by that time, be your own perspective). You see trees, but trees are not the kinds of input that would have the effect that is your friend's behaviour. Then you see the grizzly; this is exactly the kind of input that would have such an effect. Thus, generating and testing hypotheses about the cause of your friend's behaviour leads you to attribute to him the belief that there are grizzly bears ahead, and, of course, to acquire that belief yourself.[1]

Gordon's case is simple in that it does not matter who is doing the thinking. Whichever of you happens to do it on this occasion would be determined by which of you sees the grizzly first. Gordon calls such cases instances of 'total projection' (Gordon 1992: 102). I will adopt Peter Goldie's term, and call these 'base cases'. Goldie defines 'base cases' as instances of perspective-shifting in which '(i) there are no relevant differences in the psychological dispositions of A, the person attempting to empathize, and of B, the target of the attempt; in particular, both A and B are minimally rational; (ii) there are no relevant non-rational influences on B's psychological make-up or decision-making process'[2] (Goldie 2011: 307). Applied to our example: (i) both you and your friend are disposed, when walking trails, to avoid grizzly bears and both can think through ways of doing this; and (ii) neither of you are prone to panic and such in the face of grizzly bears. Whichever of you sees the grizzly first would go through the same steps, both mental and physical, as would the other one.

According to Gordon, base cases are the 'default option' for simulation. As I hope to have made clear, these generally go on under the level of consciousness. The claim is that they are part of the way in which we negotiate the world; we do not (as the theory theorists maintain) interpret our friend's behaviour by fitting it under some general psychological law; we simply, in imagination, look at the world through his eyes and 'generate and test' options for the thoughts he is having. I will return to discussion of simulation that goes on beneath our conscious awareness in the next chapter. For the remainder of this chapter I will discuss a notion of simulation that happens above the level of consciousness. These are occasions in which we deliberately set about trying to look at the world through the eyes of another, in order to find out what is going on in their heads and predict what it is that they might do.

It is worth noting that this is a quite different project from that we have been discussing. The previous example concerned the way in which we 'mind-read'; the way in which we all the time and everywhere relate to other people. The following example is something that, if it happens at all, only happens occasionally – that is, a situation in which we deliberately set out to imagine ourselves occupying the perspective of someone else. It might be that such a project turns out to be incoherent, or for some other reason impossible or unlikely. If so, that would not necessarily affect the claims made above. We could be wrong in thinking that we can empathize with others in the sense that we would be successful in imagining what it is like to be them, without being wrong in thinking that simulation is a better account of interpersonal understanding than is theory theory.

Imagine that you are sitting inside a restaurant and you notice a friend of yours, who you know to be rather careful with money, looking at a copy of the menu in the window. You are interested to know whether he will come in or walk on. You have another copy of the menu on the table in front of you. In this case, it is not a matter of there being a train of thought to go through where it is irrelevant who goes through it. Here it makes a great deal of difference: the empathizer and the target differ. The empathizer is in a different situation, has different beliefs and different dispositions to the target. Any one of these could influence how the train of thought is conducted. Nonetheless, from what has been said before, let us assume that we imaginatively adopt the perspective of our friend outside, run through the train of thought, and emerge with the decision that he would make.

This is fine; however, it is not really clear what that amounts to in detail, and the details matter. The description covers at least three different possible scenarios: what Goldie calls 'imagining-how-it is', 'in-his-shoes perspective-shifting', and 'empathetic perspective-shifting' (Goldie 2011: 305–6, 302). I shall consider each in turn.

We can imagine how it is for someone, without imagining the situation from their perspective. That is, imagining-how-it-is does not require perspective-shifting. We can imagine how it is to be a soldier waiting to engage the enemy: the tension, the unwillingness to talk, the feeling of time both passing too quickly and too slowly. We do not need to imagine how it is *from the perspective of the soldier*; we can simply imagine how it is. Similarly, we can imagine how it is to be outside, unsure of whether or not to go in, with the wind blowing around one's ears. This does not require that we take the perspective of our friend examining the menu.

Here is how Goldie characterizes in-his-shoes perspective-shifting and empathetic perspective-shifting:

> Roughly and intuitively, the difference between in-his-shoes perspective-shifting and empathetic perspective-shifting lies in the content of the imaginative project: who, in the imaginative project, is doing the thinking. So if A is wondering what B will decide in some situation, it will be in-his-shoes perspective-taking if A imagines himself in that situation, imagines himself deliberating and deciding what to do...In contrast it will be empathetic perspective-shifting if A imagines being B in that situation, deliberating and deciding what to do. (Goldie 2011: 305)

In the case of straight in-his-shoes perspective-shifting, you imagine yourself being outside, looking at the menu, and deciding what to do. In the case of empathetic perspective-shifting, you imagine that you are your friend, and, within the scope of that imaginative project, you look at the menu and decide what to do. The first of these is unproblematic; we have already seen that we can imagine ourselves in situations we are not in fact in. However, it appears that it will not do for our purposes here; we are not interested in what *we* would do were we outside looking at the menu (we already know that), we are interested in what *our friend will do*. It seems as if we need the second approach to serve our turn. The second approach, however, seems the more puzzling the more one thinks about it. What is it to imagine being someone else? In a famous discussion of the topic, Bernard Williams questioned whether the attempt to do so even makes sense:

> For suppose I conceive it possible that I might have been Napoleon – and mean by this that there might have been a world which contained a Napoleon exactly the same as the Napoleon that our world contained, except that he would have been me. What could be the difference between the actual Napoleon and the imagined one? All I have to take to him in the imagined world is a Cartesian centre of consciousness; and that, the real Napoleon had already. Leibniz,

perhaps, made something like this point when he said to one who expressed the wish that he were King of China, that all he wanted was that he should cease to exist and there should be a King in China. (Williams 1966: 42–3)

We can make the point another way. Napoleon, we can safely assume, did not believe that he was Derek Matravers. Hence, if I am successful, I would not retain the belief that I was Derek Matravers. Apart from sounding as if my imagination has gone dangerously far, if I did not retain that belief, how am I (Derek Matravers) to learn anything about what it is like to be Napoleon?

Not everyone accepts that 'empathetic perspective-shifting' is conceptually problematic. Amy Coplan gives a different characterization; the terms she uses are 'self-oriented perspective taking' and 'other-oriented perspective taking'. Presumably, by 'other-oriented perspective taking' she means something weaker than Goldie's 'empathetic perspective shifting'; weak enough not to run into the conceptual problems Williams describes.

In self-oriented perspective-taking, a person represents herself in another person's situation. Thus if I engage in self-oriented perspective-taking with you, I imagine what it's like for me to be in your situation...In other-oriented perspective-taking, a person represents the other's situation from the other person's point of view and thus attempts to simulate the target individual's experiences as though she were the target individual. (Coplan 2011: 9–10)

To illustrate the complexity, I shall mention another distinction, this time by Shaun Nichols and Stephen Stich, which, although part of the same discussion, cuts across the ones just made. They distinguish 'actual-situation-simulation', in which 'the predictor simulates the target after first putting himself in a situation which is very similar to the target's' (Stich and Nichols 1997: 302), and their favoured view, 'pretence-driven off-line simulation', in which 'pretend' inputs (corresponding to the target's actual inputs – the 'make-beliefs' I discussed earlier) are fed into 'decision-making or practical reasoning mechanisms' that are taken offline (Nichols and Stich 2003: 132). Depending on how various key claims are interpreted, both of these seem to accommodate both of Goldie's 'in-his-shoes' and 'empathetic' perspective-shifting, and also both of Coplan's 'self' or 'other' oriented 'perspective taking'.

So as not to get dragged into having to keep track of an increasing number of fine distinctions, I shall adopt Goldie's way of dividing the territory, although I will return to Nichols and Stich's view at the end of the next chapter. What we need, then, is 'in-his-shoes-perspective-shifting'. There are still problems, however. The case we are considering differs from the base case in both of the ways Goldie describes above. First, although we can assume that you and your friend are minimally rational, you do have different psychological dispositions. You are disposed to spend money; your friend is disposed not to spend money. Furthermore, there might be many psychological differences you do not know about. Even if these factors can be accommodated by exercising care in your adopting his perspective (as we shall see shortly), differences in psychological disposition place a limit on the success of your imagining being your friend. There are some human dispositions which themselves enter into a person's reasons for action. For example, someone who possesses the virtue of being just will act a certain way in order to be just. However, there are many human dispositions that are not like this: a modest person does not act a certain way in order to be modest and a meek person does not act a certain way in order to be meek. Plausibly, in our example, a carefulness with money is more likely to be the second sort of disposition rather than the first.[3] If so, it is difficult to see how you can simulate your friend's thoughts. For them, carefulness with money is part of the non-conscious background to their thinking. For you, it is consciously guiding the perspective you adopt. As Goldie puts it, 'A cannot, as part of a consciously willed project, keep B's characterization in the non-conscious background in her imaginative exercise of wondering what B will decide to do in a certain situation' (Goldie 2011: 309). The situation is not much better with respect to the failure of the second of Goldie's criteria for being a base case. There may well be non-rational influences on B's decision-making. He could be very hungry, he could particularly like cassoulet (which the restaurant is advertising as their signature dish), or he could be influenced by the colour of the menu or the choice of the font. Even if you know about some of these things, it would be difficult to assign the right weights to them. B himself might not know how much he will be influenced by a desire for cassoulet; perhaps he finds that, on this particular evening, he has a yen for something oriental rather than something French.

There are two replies an empathy theorist could make to this raft of problems. The first is to restrict the scope of the claim that we learn the contents of another's mind by simulation. This is vividly illustrated by Jane Heal with the example of anticipating someone's state of mind on drinking half a bottle of whisky. I might be able to predict what they are going through theoretically (I know of the effects of alcohol) or by calling to mind what it was like for me last time I performed that rash action. It will not help, however, for me to imagine myself in their situation; that will not re-create in me what they are going through. For the reasons we have canvassed (and, as we shall see, for reasons which flow from her construal of what is really at issue), Heal narrows the scope of the claim to a subset of the base cases:

> The only cases that a simulationist should confidently claim are those where
>
> (a) the starting point is an item or collections of items with content;
> (b) the outcome is a further item with content; and;
> (c) the latter content is rationally or intelligibly linked to that of the earlier item(s). (Heal 1996a: 76)

This would severely restrict the domain in which we could take simulation to be a reliable method of reading other minds. In essence, it would be a method of attributing to others the conclusions that could be drawn from collections of propositions. This would go beyond the conclusions of deductive arguments as Heal allows the conclusions to be 'rationally or intelligibly linked', where 'intelligibly linked' will allow inductive and probabilistic reasoning. However, the scope would be disappointingly narrow. We should note, however, that Heal does not say that simulation does not happen in a broader spectrum of cases, only that the simulationist should not 'confidently claim' that it does. Indeed, she does not say that 'it is impossible that there should be psychological simulation involving non-content or non-intelligible linkages'; rather, 'there can be no a priori assumption in favour of the existence of such cases' (Heal 1996a: 77). I will give a fuller explanation of the rationale for her making these claims in the next chapter.

This opens the way to a second reply on behalf of the empathy theorist. We have considered and rejected the idea that we imagine that we are our friend. We have also considered and rejected the idea that we can, reliably, imagine taking on our friend's dispositions and desires, and deliberate from the perspective of someone with those dispositions and desires. However, we could limit our ambitions even further. Indeed, Goldie calls this way 'unambitious in-his-shoes perspective shifting' (Goldie 2011: 311). We accept that we are not able to re-create our friend's mind in our own. Instead, we simulate being in their situation, discover what we would do, and then correct for the differences we know there are between us. That is, having shifted our perspective, we make various 'corrections': we factor into our deliberations that the deliberator is careful with money, what we know of the deliberator's food preferences or what the state of their appetite might be. Robert Gordon calls this 'patching' our shift of perspective (Gordon 1992: 106–15).

This more modest perspective-shifting seems possible. We do not imagine of ourselves that we are careful with money or that we have a desire for cassoulet. Rather, we imagine examining the menu, and then we correct for differences ('Well, I would probably come in but my friend might find it a bit expensive'). The conclusion, however, is modest; it does not promise some startling route to understanding other people. Furthermore, it is epistemically risky; we have first to know what the relevant differences are between ourselves and the target, and then we have to be accurate in our assessment of the way in which those differences will influence their deliberations. We have established some ground for simulation theory nonetheless. It is secure if we are simulating content which is rationally or intelligibly linked, and we can stretch to predicting the outcome of others' deliberations in wider circumstances – although we need to recognize our fallibility when we do so.

I began this chapter by setting up the debate between theory theory and simulation (or 'empathy') theory. As simulation is a general account of how we learn what goes on in the heads of others, it is something that we do all the time more or less unconsciously. I considered an example of this (you and your friend walking along the track), which (as it happened) was also an example of the 'generate and test' method of simulation. However, this is not the only phenomenon that has been discussed under the heading of 'simulation' in discussions of empathy. Thus, I went on to consider attempts at empathy in which we deliberately set out to discover what someone is thinking and how that person might act. Having now staked out the ground, and raised a number of problems, I shall, in the next chapter, return to the discussion of 'mind-reading'. I shall try to clarify the nature of the claims that are being made as different theorists put forward quite different types of account. I shall examine Jane Heal's arguments that the claims are a priori: that something like empathy or simulation follows from our general thoughts about interpersonal understanding. In contrast, Alvin Goldman and others take themselves to be putting forward a posteriori claims – empirical hypotheses about the way the mind works. I will then look at some exciting developments that are being made in the brain sciences, before making some general observations about the relation between the contributions philosophy and cognitive sciences can make to this debate.

4
A Priori and
A Posteriori Empathy

In the last chapter I gave some arguments for thinking that simulation theory was to be preferred to theory theory as an account of interpersonal understanding. As I indicated, there is not the space in this book to follow the labyrinthine twists and turns of the debate so we will have to be content with an approach that takes a broad brush, but that I hope picks out some interesting features. It is not part of my argument that interpersonal understanding is devoid of theoretical elements, or that the division between simulation and theory theory is particularly clear. It is rather that everyday interpersonal understanding has some interesting role for something like empathy. If this is true then, unlike the case of consciously imagining ourselves into the perspectives of others, it will be something that happens below the level of conscious experience; it will be something we do, automatically, much of the time.

This chapter is structured around a question of the status of the simulationist claims. There are two options. The first option holds that some kind of simulationist account would follow from a clear grasp of the way in which we understand each other. In other words, some kind of simulationist account is simply the correct description of our actual practices. If this were the case, the account would (in some sense) be a priori. I have already adduced some a priori considerations in favour of simulation theory; in the last chapter, I argued on purely philosophical grounds that simulation theory is supported by the fact that we have no theory of relevance. The second option holds that it is an open question how we understand each other. Interpersonal understanding could use theory-theory mechanisms or it could use simulationist mechanisms. Deciding which of these is appropriate involves careful consideration of the evidence, from philosophy, psychology and neuroscience. If the matter is to be decided empirically, then, of course, it would be necessary to find some way of sorting out a theory of relevance. The literature that takes the second option is a great deal more multifaceted than that which takes the first. Hence, my discussion of the second option will cover more ground. I will first consider the most prominent statement of the view that the question as to whether we use theory theory or simulation can be answered by a careful weighting of the evidence. I will then consider some of the exciting scientific discoveries that, it is claimed, have a bearing on the debate. Finally, I will move on to consider some attempts to fit empathy into a well-known research programme that is attempting to provide a 'cognitive architecture' of the mind.

Jane Heal has argued that it is a priori that, in the case of mental states with content, simulation, or something akin to simulation, occurs. For some, there will be a short way of dealing with this claim. For them, the notion of the a priori has its place only for claims amenable to proof in a formal system. To appeal to the notion outside such a context is to use intuition-mongering as part of proper enquiry. Heal is aware of this problem, and makes clear that by holding that a claim is 'a priori' she does not mean that the claim could never be dropped, nor that she is committed to dubious notions of analyticity, nor to there being a sharp distinction between philosophy and science. Rather, she means that the claim is 'deeply embedded in our world view' and that 'if challenged, we are thoroughly at a loss to describe realistically or in any detail how we would carry on intellectually if we could not rely on it' (Heal 1988: 94). In other words, she is at least attempting to use the notion shorn of its unappealing metaphysical baggage.

Heal's focus is on 'predicting others' future psychological states and actions on the basis of knowledge about their current psychological states' (Heal 1996b: 45). Her central argument is straightforward, but nonetheless important. Consider what would occur when thinking about things happening in our immediate environment; say, being in an unfamiliar kitchen and working out how to make a cup of coffee. We open cupboards to work out where the coffee is, we work out how to put the coffee-maker together, we come up with and test some plausible hypotheses about how to turn the hob on and so on. Now consider this hypothetically: what we *would* do *were* we in an unfamiliar kitchen working out how to make a cup of coffee. Heal's point is that when we think about possibilities, we do not employ a body of thought that has some special contents that are about possibilities; we employ thoughts with the same contents as we use in the actual case. Similarly, when we think about what others think, we generally do not employ a body of thought consisting of thoughts about what others think. (The caveat – 'generally' – is in there because, of course, the fact that we are thinking about another person thinking about something *might* introduce something that would not be there if it were simply us thinking about that thing.) In general, when we think about others thinking about something, we employ mental states with the same content as the person doing the thinking.

Heal makes her point with a helpful analogy of understanding photographs. When I am attempting to understand photographs of vegetables, I do not employ some special 'photograph-specific body of knowledge' concerning the appearance of vegetables. Rather, I simply employ my standard knowledge about what vegetables look like:

> Here what makes it possible for grasp on the subject matter of X to be deployed as part of grasp on the subject matter of photographs of X is the usual success of photographs in accurately capturing the appearance of what they represent. But might it be the case that we do not, in fact, rely on this at all but instead produce our predictions about the appearance of photographs of X by calling upon an entirely separate and photograph-specific body of information? In certain cases, those where photographic accuracy fails, a good grasp of what photographs of X are like may indeed require possession

of information which has nothing to do with what X is like but is specific to photographs of X. Perhaps turnips emit strange rays which produce black-and-white zigzags on any film exposed to them. More realistically, there are effects like the pink eyes which flash photographs often endow us with. But the idea that all competence in thinking about what photographs look like is sustained by such photograph-specific bodies of information is surely not worth serious contemplation. Among other difficulties, it postulates an immensely wasteful duplication of bodies of knowledge, and it fails to explain why someone acquiring knowledge about the appearance of a new kind of thing automatically acquires abilities to think about the appearance of photographs of that sort of thing. (Heal 1988: 101)

To distinguish her view from other, broader, notions of simulation, Heal adopts the term 'co-cognition'; 'the everyday notion of thinking about the same subject matter' (Heal 1988: 97). In thinking about you thinking about some subject matter X, I do not call upon an entirely separate body of information about 'other-people-thinking-about-X'. Rather, I simply call upon my body of information about X. As far as the relations between the contents go, it does not matter who does the thinking. The question is 'What conclusion would A come to?' where A ranges over all rational agents, including you or me (see also Goldie 2011: 308). If I want to know what conclusion you will come to, given some evidence, all I need to know is what conclusion I would come to were I given the same evidence. I do not need to call upon thoughts embodied in some psychological theory to enable me to grasp what you would think.

Heal summarizes her claim as follows:

It is an a priori truth that thinking about others' thoughts requires us, in usual and central cases, to think about the states of affairs which are the subject matter of those thoughts, namely to co-cognise with the person whose thoughts we seek to grasp. (Heal 1988: 99)

We are now in a position to better understand Heal's restriction of simulation to mental states with content, as discussed in the last chapter. This is because her central argument simply is about thinking thoughts with the same content as the target:

> Let us [consider an] example in which the other believes that p_1-p_n and is interested in whether or not q. I know this and I am interested in whether or not she comes to believe that q. What she will do is wonder 'In the light of p_1-p_n is it the case that q?' that is, she will direct her thought to answering the question whether q, having in mind the evidence that p_1-p_n. If the propositions that p_1-p_n imply that q, and she comes to be aware of them as so doing, then she will come to believe that q, taking this to be a belief to which she is entitled, in the light of the facts (as she sees them) that p_1-p_n. What will I do? If I share her beliefs I may, in effect, pose myself just the same question, viz., 'In the light of the facts that p_1-p_n is it the case that q?' But if I do not share her beliefs, then the question I should address is, rather, 'If it were that p_1-p_n would it be that q?' But in either case the other person and I share a central aim, namely trying to get a sense of the relations of implication or otherwise between p_1-p_n and q. We carry out this aim by exercising our ability to think about the subject matters of p_1-p_n and q. And if it comes to seem to me that if it were that p_1-p_n then it would be that q, then I attribute to the other the belief that q. (Heal 1998: 38)

Co-cognition is restricted to content, because it is only content that, in the relevant sense, can be shared. If Heal's argument is correct, which it surely is, then empathy (in some sense) is needed to understand the minds of others and predict their behaviour. We do not have a theoretical understanding of what the target is thinking (although theoretical elements could enter in); rather, we replicate their thoughts – in Heal's terminology, we 'co-cognize' with them.

The fact that simulation (in the form of co-cognition) has been established a priori makes problematic the debate between Heal and her interlocutors. Inasmuch as both sides were attempting to establish broadly the same thesis, they will have been working at cross purposes. Being established a priori, simulation (in its co-cognition version) is not up for empirical proof or disproof. This is not to say that there could be no role for empirical enquiry; there is still the matter of how co-cognition actually occurs: 'what is up for scientific investigation is not whether this sort of simulation [co-cognition] plays an important role, but rather the exact boundaries of that role and how the simulation is realized or embodied' (Heal 1988: 92). However, it is not clear that both sides are attempting to establish broadly the same thesis. I said above that Heal's focus was on 'predicting others' future psychological states and actions on the basis of knowledge about their current psychological states', which she explicitly distinguishes from '[arriving] at judgements about others' thoughts, feelings, and so on from knowledge of their placement in the environment or bodily behaviour' (Heal 1996b: 45). She is even more explicit about the difference in a later paper: ' "Simulation" (understood as coming to a view about what another thinks or will do by seeking to recreate his or her train of thought) is neither a necessary element of, nor something which occurs only in the context of . . . deliberative co-cognition' (Heal 2013: 350).

This is one of those places in the debate where it is useful to distinguish between different senses in which the word 'simulation' is being used. Heal says that her key claims 'deserve the label "simulationist claims" if we take likeness or resemblance to be a form of "simulation" ' (Heal 1988: 107). Co-cognition is a matter of the simulator simply thinking about the same subject matter, sharing content with the target. We can now see why Heal issued a warning about her analogy, quoted earlier, between using a model aircraft in a wind tunnel to learn about an actual aircraft and using our own minds to 'model' the minds of others. When we co-cognize, we are not *simulating* the target's mental states in the sense of creating a second 'pretend' set of mental states. Rather, we are thinking along with them. This would be an instance of what Shaun Nichols and Stephen Stich refer to as 'actual-situation-simulation' (although, as we have seen, that term covers all cases in which the focus is on the train of thought of the simulator, rather than the target, which includes 'in-his-shoes-imagining') (Nichols and Stich 2003: 133). Simulation, in a broader sense than that meant by 'co-cognition', may well be amenable to empirical investigation. As we have seen, Heal herself seems open to the suggestion that there is a role for something called 'simulation' that goes beyond co-cognition – it is only that 'there can be no a priori assumption in favour of the existence of such cases' (Heal 1996a: 77; see also Stueber 2006: 150–1).

I propose, then, to accept Heal's argument for co-cognition and look at whether there are a posteriori reasons for thinking that interpersonal understanding is served by simulation in some broader sense.[1] Philosophers interested in empathy (particularly from the United States) have done much to explore the rich empirical work coming from the cognitive sciences and show how they are relevant to the debate. A landmark in this enquiry is Alvin Goldman's book, *Simulating Minds: The Philosophy, Psychology, and Neuroscience of Mindreading* (Goldman 2006). Goldman surveys an impressive range of scientific evidence and concludes that it favours 'a hybrid account' of mind-reading. Such an account allows a place for some theorizing during the process of simulation, but it is basically simulationist in nature.

Goldman's account is organized around the distinction between what he calls low-level simulation and high-level simulation. This does not correspond to the distinction I have been using between processes of which we are not aware and processes of which we are aware. 'Low-level simulation', is, for Goldman, 'comparatively simple, primitive, automatic, and largely below the level of consciousness'. These are processes, such as 'face-based emotion recognition', that are primitive in at least two ways:

> Reading basic emotions has special survival value, so specialized programs may have evolved for emotion recognition that don't operate in other mindreading domains. In addition, emotion reading may be based on a type of process – a mirroring process – that is cognitively fairly primitive, whether or not it is innate and whether or not it evolved for emotion detection. (Goldman 2006: 113)

By contrast, simulation of 'mental states of a relatively complex nature, such as propositional attitudes' count as 'high level' even if they happen below the level of consciousness (Goldman 2006: 147). Hence, Heal's co-cognition, although (in a sense) simple, automatic and below the level of consciousness, will count as high-level simulation as it deals with propositional attitudes.

Goldman presents his project as an enquiry that draws on several sources: 'the present book...develops, refines, and defends simulation theory (at least a hybrid form of simulation theory), appealing to a wide range of evidence from philosophy, psychology, and cognitive neuroscience' (Goldman 2006: 4). Despite the focus being on empirical work, it is worth noting the mention of 'philosophy' here, and that Goldman himself appears to have no quarrel with the co-cognition thesis – which, because it deals with propositional attitudes is an instance of high-level simulation – and endorses it on broadly a priori grounds (Goldman 2006: 175–8). His account of high-level simulation, even if it incorporates co-cognition, certainly goes beyond it. Indeed, it includes much that is recognizably similar to that discussed in chapter 3. High-level simulation includes attempts to grasp the thoughts and predict the actions of a target by consciously imagining the world from the target's perspective, taking into account his or her character and situation. Amongst the empirical arguments that Goldman gives for this position is a failure of 'quarantine'. In order for high-level simulation of this sort to result in an accurate simulation of another's thoughts, I would need to put aside (to 'quarantine') those desires, preferences and the like of mine that I know do not belong to the target. If this version of simulation theory were correct, we would expect there to be errors which stem from a failure to 'quarantine' our own desires, preferences and the like. Consider, once again, the example in which I am trying to predict whether my friend will come into the restaurant. I imagine being in his shoes, reading the menu. There are certain preferences I have – for French food, for example – which I fail to quarantine, even though I have no evidence that my friend likes French food. Hence, I end up mistakenly predicting he will come in to order cassoulet. Goldman claims that we find exactly the kinds of failure of quarantine we would expect were simulation theory correct (Goldman 2006: ch.7; see also Stich and Nichols 1997).

I shall not get into the minutia of the debate as to how to interpret the evidence that Goldman adduces, and the extent to which it favours a simulation-based hybrid theory. Part of the difficulty is that Goldman's opponents also favour a hybrid theory, but one in which the emphasis is on theorizing rather than simulating. Hence, the differences are not clear-cut (Carruthers 2006).[2] Instead, I shall attempt to draw some more general lessons as to the relation between empirical evidence and philosophical enquiry by looking at Goldman's discussion of low-level simulation. When engaged in low-level simulation, I 'mirror' some aspect of yours and by this means discover what you are thinking or how you will act. In support of this, Goldman cites evidence that people who were unable to experience certain mental states appear to be unable to recognize them in others. The most intriguing material, however, is that concerning the fact that what is happening in the brain of the simulator appears to bear some resemblance to what is happening in the brain of the simulated (Goldman 2006: ch.6).

The notion that our inner states 'mirror' the inner states of others and, on such a basis, we attribute mental states to others without the need for inference takes us back to Lipps's original use of *Einfühlung*. As noted earlier, Karsten Stueber refers to this as 'basic empathy': 'Mechanisms of basic empathy have to be understood as mechanisms that underlie our theoretically unmediated quasi-perceptual ability to recognize other creatures directly as minded creatures and to recognize them implicitly as creatures that are fundamentally like us' (Stueber 2006: 20). According to Goldman, it is not only that we have the ability to recognize others as like-minded or like us, but that we are able to recognize (say) the specific emotion someone is feeling without conscious effort on our part. Many think the key to such an ability consists of so-called 'mirror neurons'. These, it is thought, explain the relation between our automatic, low-level, processes and our understanding of each other. The discovery of mirror neurons caused a great deal of excitement in both scientific and non-scientific communities. Although Goldman stops short of claiming that mirror neurons themselves are a sufficient basis for the attribution of mental states, he does think that 'wherever there is mirroring, the potential for simulation-based mindreading is there' and, furthermore, that humans 'exploit this potential extensively' (Goldman 2006: 140).

In the early 1990s, a group of neurophysiologists at the University of Parma discovered that certain neurons in the motor areas of the brain had a surprising property. They became active not only when a subject performed a given action, but when that subject saw that same action performed by some other subject. Some of my neurons that become active when I grasp a cup also become active when I see you grasp a cup. This looks to be a straightforward case of simulation: the observer's brain exhibits some of the same neural patterns as the brain of the observed. What is more, this mirroring occurs below the level of conscious processing. In Stueber's words, it is a 'quasi-perceptual ability'; I only have to look at you to know what you are thinking.

The discovery of 'mirror neurons' caused a great deal of excitement. When the news broke, the neuroscientist V. S. Ramachandran wrote: 'I predict that mirror neurons will do for psychology what DNA did for biology: they will provide a unifying framework and help explain a host of mental abilities that have hitherto remained mysterious and inaccessible to experiments.'[3] A book on the topic, one of whose authors led the original Parma team, opens with the claim by Peter Brook, the noted theatre director, that the discovery of mirror neurons provides the 'sharing' that takes place between actor and audience with 'a biological explanation' (Rizzolatti and Sinigaglia 2008: ix).

It looks as if mirror neurons provide us with all we need; proof that we are empathetic animals and that the empathy account of interpersonal understanding is correct (note, however, that Goldman's claims are nothing like as dramatic as those made here; see also Krznaric 2014). The key claim to investigate, for our purposes, is the following:

> Even if they involve different cortical circuits, our perceptions of the motor acts and the emotive reactions of others appear to be united by a mirror mechanism that permits our brain to immediately understand what we are seeing, feeling, or imagining others to be doing, as it triggers the same neural structures (motor or visceromotor respectively) that are responsible for our own actions and emotions. (Rizzolatti and Sinigaglia 2008: 190)

What is it for the brain to 'understand' something? This is not a trivial point about how to use words, as claiming that the 'brain understands' makes it look as if the fact that one person's neurons fire in a similar pattern to those of another is sufficient for the first person to understand the second. However, that is the point at issue: what exactly is the relation between the activation of mirror neurons and understanding? There is an optimistic and a pessimistic way of interpreting the findings about mirror neurons. The optimistic way is that mirror neurons are sufficiently tied to interpersonal understanding to support the view that simulation is what grounds interpersonal understanding. The pessimistic view is that mirror neurons are simply something that happens in the brain at a much more primitive level than is merited by any talk of understanding. That is, even given the facts about mirror neurons, all the work still needs to be done to attribute intentions and it is an open question as to whether that work is done by simulation, theory theory, or some other alternative.

The optimistic view would be boosted if it could be shown that mirror neurons were not simply reactions to movement deep within the brain, but discriminated between 'mere' movements and intentional movements. That is, it would benefit the optimist if it could be shown that mirror neurons already encoded whether there are intentions present in the observed actions. Marco Iacoboni and colleagues performed experiments in which three pairs of videos were shown to a number of observers. The first pair showed a number of objects laid out on the table as if someone were about to have tea, and a number of objects laid out on the table as if someone had just finished tea. The second showed a mug on its own, being grasped by a hand first in a whole-hand prehension and second in a precision grip. The third pair showed a combination of the first and the second: the first of the third pair showed the same hand grasping the mug in a whole-hand prehension from a table laid out for tea, and the second of the third pair showed the same hand grasping the mug in a precision grip from a table that looked as if tea had just been finished. Call these three videos A(i) and A(ii), B(i) and B(ii), and C(i) and C(ii) respectively. The experimenters found systematic differences in mirror neuron activity. In particular, the activation of the dorsal portion of the posterior section of the right inferior frontal gyrus (the frontal node of the mirror neuron system) was greater when observers were watching C then when they were watching either A or B.

Furthermore, there was different mirror neuron activity when they were watching C(i) than there was when they were watching C(ii) (Rizzolatti and Sinigaglia 2008: 125–7). Why should this matter?

Optimists about mirror neurons claim that the only relevant difference between video C and videos A and B is that video C depicts an intentional action. To quote Rizzolatti and Sinigaglia, 'the third video showed the same hand and the same prehension forms but this time in context, so as to suggest the intention of picking the mug up to [C(i)] carry it to the lips or [C(ii)] to clear it off the table' (Rizzolatti and Sinigaglia 2008: 125). If the only relevant difference between videos A and B and video C is that C depicts intentional activity, then, as the pattern of mirror-neuron firing in C differs from the pattern of neuron firing in A and B, it looks as if mirror neurons do discriminate between 'mere' movements and intentional movements. Furthermore, if C(i) and C(ii) depict actions performed with different intentions, then, as the pattern of mirror neuron firing in C(i) differs from the pattern of neuron firing in C(ii), it looks as if mirror neurons discriminate between actions performed with different intentions. If your neurons fire in a particular way when you move to pick up a mug to drink, and if my neurons fire in that way when I observe you, that strengthens the case for talk of mirror neurons being the way in which I grasp your intention.

Has the optimist proven their case against the pessimist? Does the existence of mirror neurons show that I understand you by 'mirroring' your internal states in a way that captures your intentions? It is not clear that the pessimist should be convinced. All C(i) and C(ii) do is depict a hand taking away a mug – in the context of untaken tea in C(i) and taken tea in C(ii). Certainly, this difference is marked by different patterns of activation of mirror neurons. However, what reason is there to think that these are picking up on specific intentions: the intention to raise the mug to one's lips and drink in the first instance, and the intention to clear away in the second? To take only C(i), would the pattern be the same if the intention was to feel the weight of the cup, move it closer towards the drinker, move it out of the way of the teapot or a myriad of intentions besides? Furthermore, different patterns of mirror-neuron firing will correspond to the same intention; there are many different ways of acting that result in the drinking of tea. Emma Borg (from whom I have taken these points) has argued that the optimists are committing the same error as was committed by the early behaviourists: of thinking they can take actions as functionally related – construing a set of movements as embodying the intention to take tea – without presupposing a prior grasp of that very intention (Borg 2007).

The discovery of mirror neurons was undoubtedly a great achievement. It is less clear what lessons we should draw from their discovery. Should we be optimists, and take them to show that empathy or simulation is 'hard-wired' into us? That, to use Rizzolatti and Sinigaglia's words, our brains 'understand' the intentions of others? Or should we be pessimists and take them to be an advance in our understanding of how the brain works and leave open the extent to which this contributes to our ability to read the minds of others? For all the excitement surrounding the discovery of mirror neurons, I am inclined to favour the pessimists.

A rather different approach to using the cognitive sciences to illuminate the theory-theory simulation debate has been taken by those working in the field of 'homuncular functionalism' – a view known also, by friend and foe alike, as 'boxology'. The two principal proponents, Stephen Stich and Shaun Nichols, take it as a constraint on any account of simulation that it be representable in a functionalist diagram of the cognitive architecture of the mind. They complain that the failure to adhere to this constraint means that 'cognitive mechanisms underlying pretence that have been offered by other authors are seriously incomplete' (Nichols and Stich 2003: 39).

In order to explain this approach, I will begin by sketching a widely accepted framework which relates various levels of explanation. This is owed to David Marr in his book *Vision* (1982). Consider some computation task that we might perform. Examples would be moving from the information coming in through our visual systems to information about the objects in our immediate environment, or moving from information about the behaviour of other people to information about their deliberations. Marr identified three 'levels of explanation': 'the three levels at which any machine carrying

Table 4.1   Three levels of explanation

Computational theory	*Representation and algorithm*	*Hardware implementation*
What is the goal of the computation, why is it appropriate, and what is the logic of the strategy by which it can be carried out?	How can this computational theory be implemented? In particular, what is the representation for the input and output, and what is the algorithm for the transformation?	How can the representation and the algorithm be realized physically?

out an information-processing task must be understood' (Marr 1982: 25). This is laid out in table 4.1.

At the computational level, the 'machine' (the mind) 'is characterized as a mapping from one kind of information to another, the abstract properties of this mapping are defined precisely, and its appropriateness and adequacy for the task at hand are demonstrated' (Marr 1982: 24). The second level concerns the intermediate steps of how the inputs are transformed into outputs and the final level of explanation, 'hardware implementation', considers how the 'machine' (the brain) actually works – something we can leave to the neuroscientists.

Homuncular functionalism (which from now on I shall refer to simply as 'functionalism', although readers should bear in mind that there are many different meanings to this term) describes the mind at the computational level. That is, it attempts to take something complicated, interpersonal understanding, and break it down into simpler components. Nichols and Stich, who have done most to specify the basic functional architecture of the cognitive mind, describe their procedure as follows:

> Our aim is to characterize the complex and variegated skills that constitute our mindreading capacity and to begin the job of explaining how these skills are accomplished by positing a cluster of mental mechanisms that interact with one another in the ways that we will specify. These mental mechanisms and the links between them are the 'organization of

subsystems'... Now and again we will offer some speculations of how these subsystems might themselves be decomposed into still simpler subsystems. But more often than not we will simply characterize the function of the subsystems, and their interactions, in as much detail as we can, and leave it to others to figure out how the subsystems carry out their function. Though some of the subsystems we will posit have the capacity to do very sophisticated and difficult tasks, we maintain that none of these tasks is as sophisticated or as difficult as mindreading itself. If we are right about this, then... some explanatory progress will have been made. (Nichols and Stich 2003: 11–12)

The inputs to the mechanisms will be a mixture of stuff coming from the outside, such as perceptions, and stuff coming from the inside, such as other mental states. The outputs will be other mental states and, eventually, actions. These mechanisms are often depicted in diagrams in which boxes are connected by arrows (the same manner of representation found in PowerPoint slides depicting everything from corporate structures to financial flows). The following example comes from an earlier paper by Nichols and Stich, written with Alan Leslie and David Klein:

Suppose you are told the following: 'Sven believes that all Italians like pasta. Sven is introduced to Maria, and he is told she is Italian.' Now you are asked to predict what Sven will say if asked whether Maria likes pasta. How do you arrive at your prediction?... Hypothetical inputs are fed into your own inference mechanism; the inference mechanism produces the appropriate inference given the pretend inputs; this output is then embedded in the appropriate belief sentence. So, on the above example, you feed your inference mechanism with the pretend beliefs that all Italians like pasta and Maria is an Italian. Your inference mechanism then produces the conclusion that Maria likes pasta. But this conclusion isn't fed into your belief box. Otherwise *you* would come to believe that Maria likes pasta. Rather, this conclusion is embedded in a belief sentence with Sven as the subject. Through this process, you come to believe that Sven will infer that Maria likes pasta. (Nichols, Stich et al. 1996: 43)

This is represented functionally as shown in figure 4.1.

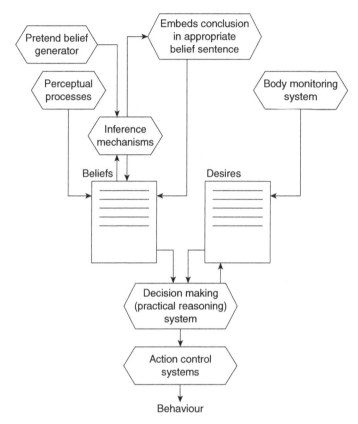

Figure 4.1   The cognitive architecture of the mind

Working through the description of the example, we can see that it corresponds to the boxes and the connections between them. At the outset, I should issue three caveats. First, it should be noted that Stich and Nichols and colleagues are not themselves endorsing empathy or simulation. Their argumentative strategy is to produce the functional representation of empathy (or simulation) and then explore whether or not it is the case (they conclude it is not – at least not in any straightforward version). Second, I am not claiming that this is the best functional representation there is. It is not even the best functional representation put forward by Stich, Nichols and colleagues (they have amended it since). Finally, the representations are not complete. Stich and Nichols have stated that 'the diagrams are intended only as crude sketches of some of the mechanisms and processes underlying various cognitive capacities, and it should be borne in mind that they do not pretend to depict all the mechanisms and processes that may affect people's actual performance' (Stich and Nichols 1997: 305). However, the figure works as an example to enable us to explore what is at issue here.

If Stich and Nichols are right, and they have identified the basic functional architecture of the cognitive mind, it would follow that any simulationist account would need to be compatible with that architecture. Hence, their complaint against philosophers who either indulge in theorizing without regard to the cognitive architecture, or who pay it some regard but fall short showing how their theories are compatible with it, would seem justified. The development of any simulationist account would have to proceed in tandem with the development of a plausible homuncular functionalism.

What response, then, could we make to Stich and Nichols? One might be to work to refine the diagram so as to make it a more plausible candidate for being a computational account of simulation. This is the approach taken by Aaron Meskin and Jonathan Weinberg. According to Stich and Nichols, the key to simulation is that 'Hypothetical inputs are fed into your own inference mechanism; the inference mechanism produces the appropriate inference given the pretend inputs; this output is then embedded in the appropriate belief sentence.' As it is 'your own inference mechanism' only one 'inference mechanism' box is needed; it is a box that delivers certain outputs given certain inputs, and it works the same way whether those inputs are beliefs or pretend beliefs. The 'single box' hypothesis might, however, not be a good explanation of some aspects of simulation. In order for the inference mechanism not to mix up what we are simulating and what we believe, it would need to be 'quarantined' from our beliefs during simulation. However, we are able to engage in belief-involving cognitions and pretend-belief-involving cognitions at the same time. Is the inference mechanism quarantined from beliefs (in order to avoid mix-ups) or not quarantined from beliefs (in order that we can run two processes simultaneously)? That is, do we need one box or two? Meskin and Weinberg use this and other considerations to argue for 'a distinct representational system in which the imagined contents are entertained'; that is, they have two boxes rather than one (Meskin and Weinberg 2006: 231).

This is one way the debate might go; towards functionalist representations that are more and more plausible mechanisms to capture the right set of boxes until, one day, we get a representation that would appear to give us everything that we want. As I said above, this would not show that we actually do use simulation, but it would at least show that simulation was possible given what we have in our heads. The functionalist method looks, on the surface at least, promising in its search for a precise picture of the basic cognitive architecture of the mind in a way that will constrain, or possibly even remove the need for, our a priori philosophical theorizing.

There is, on the other hand, space for some gentle scepticism as to whether philosophical theorizing could ever be entirely eliminated from the debate. Consider this more fundamental criticism, by Jane Heal, which would apply to the functionalist representations of both Stich and Nichols as well as Meskin and Weinberg:

[Stich and Nichols's diagram] assumes that inference is centrally a belief-to-belief matter, so that inference mechanisms operate only on beliefs, or on something which is similar enough to a belief to make the wheels of the mechanisms go round; hence the need for 'pretend beliefs' when some kind of thinking goes on which is patently not straight belief-to-belief inference. But perhaps in this respect the specific hypothesis is wrong, and inference mechanisms do not take beliefs as input but rather take items which represent or encode propositional contents without attached attitudes. Thus, working out relations of relevance, entailment, contradiction and the like between representations is one thing and done by one bit of mental machinery, while applying or withholding attitudes is a different matter, handled by some other part of the mental machinery. If this were so, then there would be no need for a person to generate a 'pretend' belief to input to her inference mechanisms when she thinks about another's beliefs. Moreover, she can input the content of the other's beliefs to those mechanisms without unhooking them or taking them 'off-line'. All she needs to do is input a content, perhaps tagging it as the content of the other's belief, not the output, and tag that too as the content of a probably further belief of the other. (Heal 1988: 110–11)[4]

At first, the criticism appears to be part of the project of searching for an adequate functional representation. As with Meskin and Weinberg, the question is only whether what is on offer is *the right* representation. The way to sort this out would be to take account of more empirical results so as to work out exactly how the boxes relate. However, Heal's point also raises a more fundamental worry. Of course, philosophical theories need to be compatible with scientific theories, and one can point to ways in which empirical findings have influenced, or determined, philosophical thinking. Few philosophers now would argue, as used to be argued, that emotions play no part in rational decision-making, as work by Antonio Damasio and others has demonstrated that emotions *do* play a part in rational decision-making (Damasio 1996). For this reason, philosophers ought to be aware of developments in the contemporary cognitive sciences. However, there are at least two lines of thought that should make us hesitate before putting all aside to pursue the functionalist approach.

The first is in specifying, and clarifying, the problem. That is, we begin by looking at the way we think and talk, and try to work out what this commits us to. What is interpersonal understanding? What does it involve? Much philosophical work needs to be done for such clarifications, on getting the right elements, and specifying the right computational set-up. As the above criticisms of specific functional proposals make clear, we are still some considerable way from even sorting out what the problem is. Second, as Kathleen Stock has argued, it is not clear that functional approaches, for all their scientific pretentions, have greater resources at their disposal than those available to the philosopher via observation and reflection (Stock 2011). The extent to which we take these to be problems for functionalism largely depends on our broader view of the philosophy of mind. For some, the mind is there to be mapped and there is a correspondence between our mental-state terms, or some more scientifically respectable successor to our mental-state terms, and what happens at Marr's third level of explanation. This at least gives us hope of a definitive functionalist representation. For others, who are less certain that the mind is out there to be mapped, this will be more problematic. Even for the optimists, we have to know which boxes to use, and what the relations are between them, and it is unclear that the process of speculating as to which boxes go where helps us understand the issues that drove us to consider these questions in the first place. In other words, constructing functional representations might be a necessary stop along the way to showing how the process can be physically realized, but it is not obviously the driver in sorting out the questions of philosophical interest. At least some important work remains to be done at the level of sorting out what computations it would be enlightening for functionalism to attempt to represent.

This largely concludes what I have to say concerning empathy as an account of interpersonal understanding. Although my discussion has only scratched the surface of the philosophical literature (I have, for example, almost entirely omitted consideration of the views of Robert Gordon), I hope it has given something of the flavour of the debates. If, as I have suggested, Heal is right in her views of 'co-cognition', then we do share the contents of what goes on in the minds of others. We can also 'catch' the moods of others via what is known as emotional contagion. Although I have not discussed it, we appear to have the 'quasi-perceptual' ability to learn the emotions of others – although I agree with those who think this is not directly underpinned by so-called 'mirror neurons'. I have been more hesitant in claiming that imagining ourselves into the perspective of others enables us to know how they think, feel and will act, although, again, some limited version of this seems possible. Even if I cannot imagine being someone else, I can imagine the world from their perspective, factoring in differences between myself and the character and situation of the target. I will pick up on many of these issues when I come to talk about empathy and the emotions in chapter 6. Before that, in the next chapter, I will look at another set of claims about taking on the perspective of others: this time, with the aim of understanding the actions of individuals in the past.

5

Re-enacting the Thoughts of Others

In this chapter we will be moving from the small scale, how one individual reads the mind of another individual, to the large scale, how we understand the past. We will look at R. G. Collingwood's theory of 'history as re-enactment'. In doing so, we will see that he pre-empts some of the thoughts already considered, and also find an argument by the contemporary philosopher, Karsten Stueber, which will provide further support for the view considered in the previous two chapters: that empathy plays some role in our understanding other people.

In chapter 3, I discussed a contrast between understanding a bicycle or a radio and understanding another human being, and we explored the thought that the methods we use for understanding the former are different from the methods we use for understanding the latter. The starting point of this chapter is understanding the past; that is, historical understanding. Does that too require a distinctive method? There is a vast philosophical background to this debate. The German philosopher Wilhelm Dilthey distinguished between the kind of explanation that features in the natural sciences, *erklären*, and the kind of explanation that features in the human sciences (of which history is one), *verstehen*. The former is a third-personal understanding while the latter is understanding of action from the actor's point of view. This requires some form of 're-living' the mental life of others, which explicitly links it to empathy as we have been discussing it (Dilthey 1979). Dilthey's work was an important contribution to hermeneutics (the theory of interpretation of all human objectifications), which we could not begin to explore within the compass of this book. Hence, we shall focus on a particular manifestation of something like this view, which is closer to the discussion of the previous two chapters: the thoughts on understanding history given by Collingwood. This, indeed, is vast enough; encompassing whether there are 'laws of history' and whether history constitutes a distinctive mode of enquiry.

Let us begin with a concrete example. What is it to understand the Battle of Waterloo? One might think that it is to know the events of the day; which troops were where, and when. However, that is clearly not enough; one would also need to know why they were where they were, when they were. Once one has asked that, several options beckon. One might answer by talking of Napoleon's escape from Elba, and the desire of the other European powers to crush him before he became too powerful. One might understand the events in terms of the playing out of economic and class interests. One might also talk of the constraints operative on the protagonists; the fact that both Napoleon and Wellington needed to organize the forces at their disposal in a way that would protect their flanks. One might also talk of Napoleon and Wellington's military strategy; their plans for emerging victorious from the encounter.

We can begin to approach this by outlining a standard model of explanation with which Collingwood's work forms a nice contrast. This is due to Carl Hempel. Hempel holds that to explain an event (say, the expansion of a soap bubble) we need to bring a particular event under a covering law. This he called 'the deductive-nomological model'.

> [Explanation] may be conceived, then, as deductive arguments whose conclusion is the explanandum sentence, E, and whose premiss-set, the explanans, consists of general laws, L_1, L_2,..., L_r and of the other statements, C_1, C_2,..., C_k, which make assertions about particular facts. The form of such arguments, which thus constitute one type of scientific explanation, can be represented by the following schema:

$L_1, L_2, \ldots, L_r$
$C_1, C_2, \ldots, C_k$

$$E$$

(Hempel 1966: 51)

The intuitive idea is quite simple. To explain the expansion of a soap bubble I need two things. First, a list of certain particular facts ('the tumblers had been immersed, for some time, in soap suds of a temperature considerably higher than that of the temperature of the surrounding air; they were put on a plate on which a puddle of soapy water had formed... etc.'). Second, a statement of laws such as gas laws, and laws covering the elastic behaviour of soap bubbles (Hempel 1962: 461). The conjunction of the first and the second entails an explanandum sentence: a sentence describing what happened. In the explanation described above, the laws are strictly universal. However, Hempel admits that some explanations are probabilistic; in such cases, $L_1, L_2, \ldots, L_r$ is replaced with statements of the form that, given X, it is highly probable that Y will happen. The conclusion is, consequently, that the explanandum sentence is highly likely to be true.

Hempel thinks that, generally, historical explanations are of this latter type:

> [S]ome historical explanations are surely nomological in character: they aim to show that the explanandum phenomenon resulted from certain antecedent, and perhaps, concomitant conditions; and in arguing these, they rely more or less explicitly on relevant generalisations. They may concern, for example, psychological or sociological tendencies and may best be conceived as broadly probabilistic in character. (Hempel 1962: 466)

For example, one might at least partially explain the Anglo-Prussian victory at Waterloo by talking of the British infantry's skill at musketry and the strategy of forming squares. There is a probabilistic law which says that, in a certain set of conditions, forming skilled marksmen into squares as a defence against cavalry will have a high probability of success. Hence, one could explain the British success at Waterloo by spelling out the conditions, evoking this probabilistic law, and concluding that there was a high probability that the British infantry would be able to resist the repeated attacks of the French cavalry.

Collingwood has a very different idea of what counts as an adequate explanation in history. Collingwood was writing some time before Hempel; his principal contribution to the philosophy of history was his book *The Idea of History*, which came out posthumously in 1946 (Collingwood died in 1943) (Collingwood 1946). It really is two books combined; the first based on lectures, and the second a set of theoretical papers. It is the latter that will interest us here. There are also some chapters on history in his autobiography (Collingwood 1978), as well as some more recently published notes discovered in the vaults of Oxford University Press (Collingwood 1999). The story of what was published when, and why, and what light the later work throws on what was published earlier is fascinating (Boucher 1997). However, it is not one that need concern us now. Indeed, to untangle Collingwood's thoughts, or even only his thoughts on history, would take a hefty volume.[1] Collingwood was prone to overstatement, to paradox, to having several stabs at solving a problem (some of these resulting in inconsistent solutions), to stipulating unusual meanings for familiar terms and other philosophical faults besides. Some of the claims he makes seem, and probably are, ludicrous. In his *Dictionary of National Biography* entry of Collingwood, his friend T. M. Knox says 'in philosophy he had visions the validity of which he did not succeed in justifying to others by argument' (Matthew 1997: 156). However, amongst his voluminous writings one can find profound insights, startling anticipations of philosophical views and gems of thought that bear much reflection. I shall be interested only in some of the ideas in the philosophy of history.

In his autobiography, Collingwood gives a synopsis of his philosophy of history and makes the following three startling claims: 'All history is the history of thought'; 'historical knowledge is the re-enactment in the historian's mind of the thought whose history he is studying'; and 'historical knowledge is the re-enactment of a past thought encapsulated in a context of present thoughts which, by contradicting it, confine it to a plane different from theirs' (Collingwood 1978: 110,

112, 114). Each of these is related to one of the key claims we made earlier: that the way in which we understand human beings differs from the way in which we understand natural objects; that empathy (or simulation or co-cognition) is an essential element to our understanding rational thought; and that, although we take on another's perspective, we do not confuse that perspective with our own. As I said above, in exploring Collingwood we will use an argument by Karsten Stueber which will reinforce the points that have been made previously.

First, to Collingwood's claim that 'all history is the history of thought'. The claim seems clearly false, and, indeed, Collingwood's attempts to support it sometimes reinforce this accusation: 'Military history... is not a description of weary marches in heat or cold, or the thrills and chills of battle or the long agony of wounded men' (Collingwood 1978: 110). That is certainly not all of military history, but surely it is part of it. However, Collingwood is pointing to a distinction which should be familiar:

> There is and can be no history of nature, whether as perceived or as thought by the scientist. No doubt nature contains, undergoes, or even consists of, processes; its changes in time are essential to it, they may even (as some think) be all that it has or is; and these changes may be genuinely creative, no mere repetitions of fixed cyclical phases but the development of new orders of natural being. But all this goes no way towards proving that the life of nature is an historical life or that our knowledge of it is historical knowledge. The only condition on which there could be a history of nature is that the events of nature are actions on the part of some thinking being or beings, and that by studying these actions we could discover what were the thoughts which they expressed and think those thoughts for ourselves. (Collingwood 1946: 302)

There is a difference between understanding why natural events occurred and understanding why humans acted the way that they did. Natural events stand in causal sequences and understanding causal sequences at least looks amenable to being understood theoretically; to being captured by the deductive-nominological model described above. In contrast, humans act for reasons and, as we saw in chapter 3, there are problems with the claim that, in understanding the reasons why people acted as they did, we employ a tacit theory. Elsewhere, Collingwood makes the contrast explicit:

> When a scientist asks 'Why did that piece of litmus paper turn pink?' he means 'On what kinds of occasions do pieces of litmus paper turn pink?' When an historian asks 'Why did Brutus stab Caesar?' he means 'What did Brutus think, which made him decide to stab Caesar?' The cause of the event, for him, means the thought in the mind of the person by whose agency the event came about. (Collingwood 1946: 214–15)

By 'the thought in the mind of the person by whose agency the event came about', Collingwood means the person's reasons for acting. Now we have the contrast between the understanding of causes and the understanding of reasons, we can move on to the core (and most controversial) part of Collingwood's thesis: that understanding a thought is a matter of re-enacting it in our minds. As I said above, in picking my way through this I shall ignore the many places where Collingwood is confused or overstates his case. Instead, I will focus on the ways in which the discussion appears to pre-empt, and strengthen, the case for empathy over theory theory.

Collingwood's account of re-enactment is succinct:

> But how does the historian discern the thoughts which he is trying to discover? There is only one way in which it can be done: by re-thinking them in his own mind. The historian of philosophy, reading Plato, is trying to know what Plato thought when he expressed himself in certain words. The only way in which he can do this is by thinking it for himself. This, in fact, is what we mean when we speak of 'understanding' the words. So the historian of politics or warfare, presented with an account of certain actions done by Julius Caesar, tries to understand these actions, that is, to discover what thoughts in Caesar's mind determined him to do them. This implies envisaging for himself what Caesar thought about the situation and the possible ways of dealing with it. The history of thought, and therefore all history, is the re-enactment of past thought in the historian's own mind. (Collingwood 1946: 215)

The first thought to pull out of this is 'this, in fact, is what we mean when we speak of "understanding" the words'. This should put us in mind of Jane Heal's account of co-cognition, explored in the previous chapter. Here is one claim made by Heal that seems particularly close to Collingwood: 'To understand a language, at a basic level, is to be disposed to have aroused in one, by another's utterance and without the need for conscious puzzling, activation of the same cognitive capacities as were exercised by the utterer in herself arriving at the thought expressed' (Heal 2010: 728). That is, to understand others' words, in this case Plato's words, draws on our own understanding of language; we 're-enact' them to ourselves.

In other places, Collingwood echoes another of Heal's points; that, in reasoning, it does not matter who does the thinking. A line of reasoning is a line of reasoning, whether thought by Plato, Collingwood, Heal or ourselves. Hence, the way to grasp what someone is thinking, if what they are thinking is a line of reasoning, is to think the same thing oneself:

> Yet if I not only read his argument but understand it, follow it in my own mind by re-arguing it with and for myself, the process of argument which I go through is not a process resembling Plato's, it actually is Plato's, so far as I understand him rightly. The argument simply as itself, starting from these premises and leading through this process to this conclusion; the argument as it can be developed either in Plato's mind or mine or anyone else's, is what I call the thought in its mediation. (Collingwood 1946: 301)

Indeed, if you cannot think it yourself you do not understand it, and the way to understand it is to think it yourself.

Karsten Stueber has claimed to find an additional argument in Collingwood; at least, an argument which is suggested by Collingwood 'in a rudimentary fashion'. He calls this 'the argument from the essential indexicality of thoughts as reasons' (Stueber 2006: 152, 161). Collingwood's suggestion comes, I think, from putting together some partial thoughts in a number of places, but is perhaps best captured in this gnomic passage:[2]

> In order, therefore, that any particular act of thought should become subject-matter for history, it must be an act not only

of thought but of reflective thought, that is, one which is
performed in the consciousness that it is being performed, and
is constituted what it is by that consciousness. (Collingwood
1946: 308)

We can begin to understand this if we understand what
the difference is between a thought and a reflective thought,
and why only the latter can 'become subject-matter for
history'. In the three or so pages prior to the above quotation,
Collingwood attempts to expound this by talking about
various 'levels' of psychological activity. At the bottom level
is 'mere consciousness'. This is merely the flow of sensations,
with no consciousness that these are related to a single mind:
the feeling of cold is merely succeeded by the feeling of warmth.
The next level up is 'thinking'; this happens when I am 'aware
of myself as something more than the immediate experience
of cold: aware of myself as an activity which has had other
experiences previously, and remains the same throughout the
differences of these experiences'. This is only 'the most rudimentary form of thought' and can develop in two directions
(Collingwood 1946: 306). First, it can grasp what the sensations were that it felt in the past (this is memory) and, second,
it can distinguish the present feeling from what that present
feeling is of (this is perception). In short, Collingwood holds
that we can be aware of ourselves as the single thing that is the
subject to a flow of sensations; we can remember sensations
and also be aware of the difference between a sensation and
that of which it is a sensation. This also involves an awareness of ourselves as thinking beings. Memory and perception
require us to be conscious and also self-conscious. However,
we do not have to be conscious that we are doing it. Hence,
Collingwood, in his rather confusing terminology, allows that
we are conscious, self-conscious, but as yet only indulging in
'unconscious thinking' (Collingwood 1946: 307). To indulge
in conscious thinking, we need to be conscious that we are
doing it; something Collingwood calls 'reflecting'.

Collingwood holds – although the arguments he provides
for this claim are poor – that there cannot be a history of
memory or perception: 'A person who should sit down to
write the history of memory or the history of perception
would find nothing to write about' (Collingwood 1946: 307).

> In order, therefore, that any particular act of thought should become subject-matter for history, it must be an act not only of thought but of reflective thought, that is, one which is performed in the consciousness that it is being performed, and is constituted what it is by that consciousness. (Collingwood 1946: 308)

The puzzle here is why Collingwood should hold this. Why is history the re-enactment of only *reflective* thought, and why cannot it include conscious and self-conscious (albeit unconscious) thought? The answer is that, as we saw above, for Collingwood history is the history of reasons for action and there is a constitutive connection between understanding someone's reasons for action and re-enacting their reflective thought.

At least, this is the answer Stueber provides on Collingwood's behalf. The core thought is that 'understanding how a thought can be a reason for someone minimally requires that we can understand how a thought can be a thought that somebody recognises as his or her own' (Stueber 2006: 162). The argument proceeds in two steps.

The first draws on 'the essential and irreducible role of first-person concepts in our cognitive system' (Stueber 2006: 162). Imagine (to draw on a well-known example due to John Perry (Perry 1979)) that I am shopping in a supermarket and notice a trail of sugar. I head off in search of the person responsible; a person whose bag of sugar has broken. I circle around, but all that happens is the trail becomes thicker. Eventually I realize that I am the person responsible; the broken bag is in my trolley. As a result, I stop looking. What explains the fact that I stop looking? The short answer is that I come to believe that I am the person responsible. It is not enough (obviously) to believe that some shopper is responsible; that would not explain why I stop looking. It would also not be enough to believe that the shopper in aisle five is responsible, unless I also believed I was the shopper in aisle five. It would not even be enough to believe that Derek Matravers was responsible, unless I also believed I was Derek Matravers. In other words, 'we can grasp as a reason only if we identify it as our own' (Stueber 2006: 162).

Our concern is not our own thoughts, however, but the thoughts of other people. What do we need to think about other people's thoughts, such that we can understand that they are reasons for action for them? We need to be in a position to grasp the other person's thoughts as standing in the same relation to them as our thoughts stand to us. Stueber puts the point as follows:

> Being told that Karsten Stueber thinks that President Clinton had an affair does not immediately constitute a reason for me to do anything unless I also recognise that it is my thought. In the same manner, I do not just have to grasp that Linda thinks that President Clinton had an affair; I also have to see that Linda thinks 'I think that President Clinton had an affair'. We have to understand how another person can relate to his or her thoughts in an essentially first-personal manner. Given the above considerations about the essential use of the first-personal pronoun, this is possible only if we conceive of her use of the I-concept on the model of my own use. Only insofar as I treat her thoughts as thoughts that could be my own – and as thoughts that would move me to draw certain conclusions if I were to integrate them in my own cognitive system were I also to entertain Linda's other beliefs – can I grasp them as her thoughts and as thoughts that constitute her reasons for her action. If I am unable to do so I would have to treat them not as thoughts of a person, but as thoughts that happen to occur in a person. (Stueber 2006: 164–5)

This argument is a priori, and hence independent of empirical considerations. To grasp what it is for something to count as the thoughts of a person requires that, in imagination, we stand in a certain relation to those thoughts: namely, to regard those thoughts as thoughts we have. In other words, in order to understand others' thoughts as reasons for actions, we need to re-enact those thoughts.

Although, following Stueber, I have developed the argument from Collingwood's views on historical explanation, the conclusion is perfectly general. That is, it is not so much about history as about understanding other people generally (perhaps this is part of what lies behind Collingwood's claim that 'the right way of investigating mind is by the methods of history' (Collingwood 1946: 209)). The background in Collingwood does highlight some other issues – some of which are welcome, and some of which we would want to disavow.

What we make of this argument depends in part on what counts as understanding someone's reasons for action. We can certainly understand Caesar's reason for action de dicto: that is, we understand *that* he crossed the Rubicon in order to challenge the power of the Senate. Is such an understanding enough? It will be for many purposes (including, perhaps, the purpose of writing history). However, it misses something, as we can see if we consider not the historian, but the anthropologist. Consider a scenario in which an anthropologist is attempting to understand a culture alien from their own. They note that when people of the culture hear a frog croak, they subsequently provide their kinsfolk with a large meal. The anthropologist can understand *that* hearing a frog croak is reason for playing host for dinner. They might even understand this as having a function, in that society, of transforming wealth into status. However, there is something they will lack which they would not lack if they were able to re-enact the thoughts of the members of the culture: if they could stand in the relation, albeit in imagination, whereby hearing a frog croak would be, for them, a reason to play host for dinner.

For Collingwood, re-enactment is on the model of 'generate and test simulation' rather than 'process simulation'. That is, we have the historical record (the outcome) and we work out what the person's reasons were that led to that outcome. As Collingwood says of a military commander, 'from the recorded account of his acts we can reconstruct in our own minds the plan of campaign which he tried to carry out' (Collingwood 1946). The first thing to note about this is that any such reconstruction is only possible if there is evidence of the person's acts. Collingwood claimed that any plan that was acted upon, but was unsuccessful, is permanently lost to history (Collingwood 1978: 70). This is clearly far too strong as there can be plenty of evidence even of unsuccessful plans (as Collingwood clearly realizes elsewhere (Collingwood 1946: 312)). However, the basic point is correct. If there is no evidence of someone's thoughts we are not able to understand their reasons for action. As we will see in the next chapter, this is one of the ways in which empathy can fail.

The second thing to note is that even if we manage to 'reconstruct in our own minds' a person's reasons for action, those reasons will not generally determine a single action. This is obviously more of a problem if we are attempting to predict what action a person will perform, given some information about their situation and character. In such circumstances, our task is to predict a single action out of a range of possible actions. Peter Goldie has stressed this point.

> In trying to predict what another person will do, it may be possible to gain a grasp of the considerations which he will believe to have a bearing on the issue, but it is a further task to predict what importance the deliberator will attach to these considerations. For in his deliberation, this is just what he is trying to decide. (Goldie 2000: 207)

In re-enactment, as we have the action and need to come up with reasons, we are in a better position. However, even if we have the reasons and the action, we may still not be in a position of grasping why *those* reasons came up with *that* action. There are limits to what even re-enactment will enable us to understand.

Finally, another of Goldie's reasons to be sceptical of taking on the perspective of another will also apply to re-enactment. We saw, in chapter 3, that adopting a first-person deliberative stance from the perspective of another, if that other has different psychological dispositions from us, is problematic. If we are timid, and the other is brave, we cannot simply re-enact their thinking, as their thinking will not include the thought of bravery and ours will. If I attempt to re-enact Wellington's thoughts as to whether or not to withdraw in the face of the charge of the Imperial Guard, I will not be able to fully occupy those thoughts, as those thoughts will only make sense if considered against a background I simply do not have. I am not able to introduce that background without being conscious of it as such, which, of course, the Iron Duke was not. To quote Goldie again, 'A cannot, as part of a consciously willed project, keep B's characterization in the nonconscious background in her imaginative exercise of wondering what B will decide to do in a certain situation' (Goldie 2011: 309).

What have we shown about explanation in history? If one has Collingwood's idiosyncratic view of the content of history – that it is the history of human plans – then re-enactment is a route to explanation in history. However, there is no reason to hold Collingwood's idiosyncratic view; indeed, Collingwood himself does not hold it consistently (Dray 1999). If one wants to understand the battle of Waterloo, one will need to understand a great deal more than the protagonists' reasons for actions on the day. There is no point in attempting to enumerate everything that is of potential interest to the historian, and there is no reason to deny that explaining much of it will require theory, including theory that conforms to the deductive-nomological model. In addition, understanding others' reasons for action will require a great deal of investigation that has nothing to do with empathy. It will require finding out about their situation and character for a start. What the argument does show, modulo the reasons for doubt given above, is that if we do want to understand another's reasons for action, we need to 're-enact' their thoughts; that is, re-think their thoughts from their perspective. As Stueber says, the argument favours 'proponents of empathy by theoretically establishing empathy as the default position for our ability to understand rational agents within the folk-psychological context' (Stueber 2006: 167). Many of these points will be picked up in the next chapter.

6

Empathy and the Emotions

I have argued that, in the current debate, 'empathy' is used to name a number of disparate phenomena, no one of which has a definitive claim on the term. So far, we have focused on the broader definition of 'empathy'; that which involves understanding the thoughts of other people. In this chapter we are going to consider the narrower definition, which links empathy specifically to the emotions (I shall call this 'narrow empathy' to contrast with the earlier 'broad empathy'). This is the sense of 'empathy' people are gesturing at when they utter such things as, 'I feel your pain'. As broad empathy and narrow empathy differ, not everything claimed about the former will be true of the latter. Indeed, there is much that will not carry over.

Even within the discussion of the narrower phenomenon there is still room for disagreement. It is not clear that there is a single psychological phenomenon here for us to investigate, hence I will pick and choose what to focus on without claiming that mine is the only sensible way to divide the territory. In her introduction to a collection that links empathy to morality (a topic discussed in the next chapter), Heidi Maibom gives a definition of what she calls '(affective) empathy'; a more formal version of that given above, in chapter 1: 'S empathizes with O's experience of emotion E in C if S feels E for O as a result of: believing or perceiving that O feels E, or imagining being in C' (Maibom 2014: 3). I would like to draw attention to three aspects of this definition on the way to offering my own.

First, for Maibom, it would be sufficient to count as narrow empathy for S to feel E as a result of perceiving that O feels E. I shall assume the weaker reading of this, namely, that we can perceive that someone feels an emotion without being aware that we are doing so. On the weaker reading, Maibom's definition would include emotional contagion under narrow empathy. In chapter 2, I included emotional contagion under broad empathy in order to accommodate Goldman's 'low-level empathy'. However, the phenomenon on which I would like to focus in this chapter is a different and richer notion. Emotional contagion occurs when, through some mechanism which makes us sensitive to those around us, we take on the emotions felt by others. For example, I perceive (whether consciously or not) that the people around me are feeling anxious and thereby come to feel anxious myself. There are two contrasts with the phenomenon I would like to discuss (which I shall from now on simply refer to as 'narrow empathy' without claiming that I have identified what is generally meant by the term): (a) emotional contagion does not involve imagining the world from the perspective of the people around you; their feeling or emotion affects you directly; and (b) emotional contagion does not necessarily involve believing that the people around you are anxious. Narrow empathy involves both imagining the world from another's perspective and believing the other is feeling some emotion.

Second, the requirement that S should feel E, where E is the emotion felt by O, raises a problem of what it is to 'feel the same emotion'. I do not mean that there is a problem as to whether the empathizer feels quantitatively the same emotion as the target (as before, I shall refer to the person to whom we feel empathy as the 'target' of our empathy). Barring some bizarre way of individuating emotions, it is clear that narrow empathy requires two instances of emotion to be felt. Rather, the problem is whether the empathizer is feeling a token of the same type of emotion as the target. There are two issues here. To make a slightly problematic distinction, the first concerns the phenomenology of the emotion and the second its intentional content. The first issue concerns whether what it is like for the empathizer to have the emotion is what it is like for the target to have the emotion. We can grasp the second issue if we consider a case in which we empathize with someone whose emotion is directed at some particular thing (for example, an unrequited love for some particular person). Does it matter that our empathetic emotion does not have that object? In other words, are we still feeling the same emotion if *we* do not feel unrequited love for that person?

Sorting out the first issue is made difficult by the fact that the identity conditions for emotional states are somewhat vague, and hence it is not clear what we need to feel in order to feel 'the same emotion'. Whilst this is not the place to attempt a fully fledged theory of emotions, there is a broad consensus that (to quote Ronald de Sousa) 'Emotions vary ... in a number of dimensions – transparency, intensity, behavioural expression, object-directedness, and susceptibility to rational assessment' (de Sousa 2014: 6). As emotions can vary in these directions, it is not clear how much difference there needs to be in what two people are feeling before we start to question whether what it is like for the first is what it is like for the second. It does not seem as if there is any way in principle of sorting this out. If the emotion in question is sadness, it seems as if what it is like for the empathizer could well be what it is like for the target. However, if the emotion in question is being desolate and broken-hearted, it seems to set too high a bar for empathy to require that what it is like for the empathizer must be just what it is like for the target – no more and no less. However, we do not want to set the bar too low either, as doing so brings with it the danger of losing the distinction between empathy and sympathy. The empathizer needs to feel something like what the target feels; they need to feel more than mere compassion for the target. It is tempting to borrow from Hume, and argue that the empathizer needs to feel an impression of what the target feels; a less vivid version of the same emotion. Provided we interpret this loosely, this seems to be the right kind of constraint. Several of the features listed by de Sousa come by degree. Thus, the empathizer and the target could have an emotion of recognizably the same type, and yet differ in degree. Whilst admitting this solution is unsatisfactorily vague, it is the one

I shall adopt. For ease of reference, I will say that what it is like for the empathizer has either to be what it is like for the target, or *akin* to what it is like for the target.

I shall argue for a similar solution to the second issue. Arguably, the cognitive content of an emotion is, in part, constitutive of its identity. What makes a mental state of anger at Janet is that it consists, in part, of some cognitive state that has as its content that I have been slighted by Janet. If the target feels a painful unrequited love for his inamorata, it would appear that the empathizer could not feel that emotion, as (we can assume) the empathizer does not have the cognitive component necessary for what he or she feels to be a token of that emotion: namely, a painful unrequited love for the inamorata in question. One solution might be for the empathizer to form an emotion that has a cognitive content with an object that has for the empathizer the same kind of status as the object of the target's cognitive content has for the target. This does not seem right. Not only is it quite possible that the empathizer does not have an object that would play an equivalent role, but it also gets the nature of the project wrong. Focusing on what would distress ourselves does not seem the right mechanism for getting ourselves into the state we want to get in – namely, focusing on what is distressing the target (Goldie 2000: 202). A better description of what is happening is that the empathizer has some of the emotions of pain and upset, or emotions akin to pain and upset in the way specified above, directed on to a baldly specified and indeterminate object: something like, 'an object that is such as to merit the kinds of emotions that the target is experiencing'. If the empathizer has been in the target's position in the past, what he or she feels is likely to be informed by memory traces of his or her emotions directed at the object that played the same role in his or her life. However, that falls short of saying that his or her emotions are now directed on to that object. I shall discuss the relation between memory traces and empathy below.

Third, even if the empathizer is feeling the same type of emotion as the target, it does not seem quite right to say (as Maibom does) that they are feeling an emotion *for* the target. In empathizing with someone who is distressed, we do not come to feel distress for that person. Rather, we come to feel distress *alongside* that person. Maibom herself is aware of the issue:

> I talk of empathy proper as an emotion that is felt for the other in addition to with them, but it is important to stress that the 'feeling for' that I have in mind is not meant to include 'concern' as a feeling or attitude felt separate from, and in addition to, the particular emotion that is felt for the other ('empathetic anger', say). The extent to which 'feeling for,' as I am using the expression here, connotes concern for another is the extent to which such a feeling or attitude is implicit in the fact that one feels an emotion that is more appropriate to the situation of the other than to one's own. 'Feeling for' is to be understood broadly so as to include cases where I am angry with a person because that person wronged you where, in a sense, you are neither the object nor the subject of my emotion. What makes it a case of empathetic anger is that I am feeling it not directly as a sort of objective moral anger, but rather I feel it on your behalf. (Maibom 2014: 5)

Quite what this amounts to is a difficult issue, and one that has not been considered as much as one might have hoped by writers on empathy (for a good discussion, plus references to what material there is, see Lopes 2011: 121–3). Kendall Walton's account, briefly mentioned in chapter 2, has this problem as its focus and holds that the empathizer uses his or her mental state as a way of referring to the mental state of the target: the target feels like *this*, where 'this' refers to the empathizer's mental state. This establishes an intentional connection between the emotion of the empathizer and the emotion of the target, in the absence of the empathizer's emotion being *for* the target (Walton 2015: 5–10). Walton's suggestion is intriguing, and seems true to much of the phenomenology of narrow empathy. If this suggestion is not the whole story, the considerations canvassed in the previous paragraph might also prove valuable here. The empathizer does not feel an emotion for the target, but the same emotion as the target with a baldly specified and indeterminate object, whose features are only those that would merit being the object of the target's emotion. Once again, the empathizer's emotion is in some sense alongside the target, without being for the target.

With these considerations in mind, I propose a definition of narrow empathy based on that given by Peter Goldie in his book *The Emotions*, although changed to take into account subsequent discussion in the literature (including discussion by Goldie (2000: 195–205)). Narrow empathy occurs when the empathizer experiences an emotion E as a result of imagining what it is like for the target, where this involves some information about the situation of the target and some information about the character of the target, and E is either the same as, or akin to, the emotion felt by the target. Maibom herself has commented that Goldie's definition is 'stringent', and 'leaves out what most people would call empathy and what most of the psychological literature regards as empathy' (Maibom 2014: 3). Some of what Maibom notes the definition leaves out was covered in earlier chapters under the heading of 'broad empathy'. To that extent, Maibom's comment is justified; this definition only covers a part of the debate. There is a more fundamental point, however. This definition suggests that narrow empathy is a very deliberate affair, with the empathizer deliberately factoring background knowledge into their imaginative project. This would indeed be 'stringent', as, intuitively, narrow empathy is not always under our voluntary control.

Does the definition imply that narrow empathy is always deliberate? For there to be non-deliberate (that is, involuntary) instances of narrow empathy two things would need to be true. First, it would need to be the case that we could exercise our imaginations non-deliberately. Second, it would need to be the case that we could factor in background knowledge about the target's situation and character non-deliberately. I shall take these in turn.

In this debate, as elsewhere in philosophy, we are hampered by there being no clear account of the imagination. The existing theories of the imagination differ as to whether the exercise of the imagination is always deliberate (Dorsch 2012). At least, the kind of exercise of the imagination that is relevant here; whether or not, for example, dreaming is an instance of imagining, has no bearing on the use of the imagination in narrow empathy. Clearly, we are able to exercise our imaginations deliberately; we can settle back for a cool hour and imagine what the world is like from some other perspective. However, there seem also to be instances where the imagination is not under our conscious control. We can find ourselves imagining things that we do not want to imagine; when listening to a story, or hearing noises from the room next door, images can appear unbidden in our minds.[1] In a similar spirit, there seem instances of perspective-taking which appear to be involuntary. Consider a parent who witnesses their child get a fright and burst into tears. It seems quite possible, even likely, that the parent can simply find him- or herself occupying, in imagination, the child's perspective. Furthermore, given that the imaginative project is under way (albeit non-deliberately), it seems clear that we are able to bring our background knowledge to bear on it. Indeed, in exercising our imaginations, we do this all the time. If I set myself to imagine what a London street was like in medieval times, I recruit a vast store of background historical knowledge to inform my project. In short, I see no reason to rule out the possibility of simply finding oneself, without deliberation, imagining what the world is like for someone where that includes recruiting beliefs about their situation and character. Consider a friend who is pouring out their heart concerning their ongoing divorce. Nothing in the listener's reaction need be deliberate; rather, the listener follows along, feeling something akin to what the target feels (shock, sadness, anger) as a result of imagining what it is like to be the target, factoring in their situation and character. In such cases, the empathizing does not seem to be a deliberate act. This suggests that we should extend what we are willing to countenance as narrow empathy to instances that are not subject to the will. This conclusion runs counter to my earlier claim that the best we can hope for, when empathizing, is 'unambitious in-his-shoes perspective-taking'. I return to this issue below.

Now we have a definition of narrow empathy we can contrast it with other phenomena that flourish in the same hedgerow. I have already distinguished it from emotional contagion in discussing Maibom's definition above. It is also distinct from sympathy. Narrow empathy and sympathy have, as one would expect, something in common: we might come to feel sympathy for the target as a result of imagining what it is like for the target, where this involves some information about the situation of the target and some information about the character of the target. That is, as a result of such an act of imagination we come to feel compassion for the person. There are still two important differences between this and narrow empathy, however. First, unlike being empathetic, to be sympathetic we do not *have* to imagine what it is like for the target. Sympathy can arise in other ways; we can simply come to feel compassion as a result of believing that the target merits such a feeling. We can come by that belief in any number of ways: by seeing the target, by listening to them, by hearing about their plight from other people and so on. Second, unlike being empathetic, when being sympathetic we do not replicate the target's emotion or something akin to that emotion. The feeling of compassion is the sympathetic response to someone who is sad, but compassion is not the same as sadness or related to sadness in an appropriate way.

Narrow empathy is also distinct from 'shared emotions', which itself is an umbrella term covering a range of different phenomena (Salmela 2012). Consider, for example, a crowd watching a rugby match at which a drop goal in the dying minutes seals a victory. The crowd roars in a shared feeling of elation. It is not obvious what the best way is to describe this. However, we could point to each member of the crowd having a common object of the emotion and a common concern. There is probably some measure of reciprocity as well; part of the joy of supporting a team is the Dionysian loss of a sense of self; what one feels is, at least in part, grounded in the belief that other people feel the same. This instance of a shared emotion differs from straightforward cases of contagion, however, as members of the crowd are aware of why they are feeling as they feel, and are aware of the cause (and the object) of their emotion. As one might expect, the phenomena grouped under the heading of 'shared emotions' have similarities to, and differences from, narrow empathy. One important similarity is that each member of the crowd feels the same emotion as another member of the crowd. An important difference, however, is that a member of the crowd does not come to feel what it is that they feel by imagining what it is like to be another member of the crowd, and the situation and character of the rest of the crowd do not enter into each member of the crowd's thoughts.

The definition I have given also suggests we need to distinguish between imagining the world from someone's point of view in a way which does factor in their situation and character, and imagining the world from someone's point of view in a way which only factors in their situation. Consider Daniel Kahneman and Amos Tversky's well-known experiment concerning counter-factual thinking (Kahneman and Tversky 1982). Two people, Mr Crane and Mr Tees, are on their way to the airport to catch different flights, which each leave at the same time. They are both delayed in traffic by thirty minutes. On arrival, Mr Crane discovers his flight left on time, while Mr Tees discovers that his was delayed, and he missed it by only five minutes. Subjects were asked who would be the most upset; 96 per cent said that it would be Mr Tees. The imaginative process leading to this judgement is, it seems fair to assume, that the subjects imagine what things are like from each of Mr Crane and Mr Tees's perspectives and find occupying the latter perspective involves more upset. Peter Goldie argues that this cannot count as narrow empathy as 'Crane and Tees are not people of whom one has a characterisation'. Instead, we are simply imagining *ourselves* missing the plane by twenty-five minutes and missing the plane by five minutes (Goldie 2000: 201). Goldie lends support to his case with the thought that, if one *did* have a characterization of Mr Tees (perhaps as being akin to Mother Teresa) this might well yield a different judgement. There does seem to be a relevant difference here. Working out which of Mr Crane and Mr Tees would be the most upset seems rather more straightforwardly an instance of hypothetical thinking: in which situation would we ourselves be more upset – missing the plane by twenty-five minutes or missing the plane by five minutes? This lacks that aspect which has dominated the discussion of narrow empathy: that of imagining, in more than a simply formal way, what it is like for some other person.

Having contrasted 'empathy' in the narrow sense with some similar phenomena, I shall attempt to fill in a little more of the detail. In discussing broad empathy, I looked at (broadly) two distinct kinds (I say 'broadly' as the base cases sit somewhere between the two). The first was exemplified by Jane Heal's notion of 'co-cognition'. This was an a priori thesis: in attempting to understand someone who is thinking about a certain subject matter, we engage our own capacities to think about that subject matter. Such a thesis was restricted to thinking about contents that were 'rationally or intelligibly linked' (Heal 1996a: 77). There might be the cases of something like co-cognition that result in the sharing of emotions. Feelings, or, more specifically, emotions, are not in general entirely distinct from our rational and intelligible thoughts. Unlike random pains or itches, we generally have reasons for feeling angry, happy or sad. Thus, in following through a train of thought the elements of which were 'rationally or intelligibly linked' we could arrive at a proposition that was intelligibly linked to feeling an emotion. Clearly, the link between thinking p and then thinking q (if p implies q) is a lot more secure than the link between thinking p and feeling happy (if p is a reason to feel happy). Furthermore, although there is only one way to think q, there are many ways to feel happy (we can be slightly happy, wistfully happy, deliriously happy and more besides). Hence, I will be a great deal more secure in replicating a target's thought from p to q if p implies q, than I will in replicating a target's thought from p to some particular tone of happiness if p is a reason to be happy. Furthermore, with propositional contents, all I need to do is to move from thinking p to thinking q. With the feelings and emotions, I need to move from thinking p not merely to thinking that the target is happy, but actually to feeling happy. None of this, however, would count as an instance of narrow empathy as one is not imagining what it is like for the target, nor is one involving information about their situation and character, so, having pointed it out, I shall put this possibility to one side.

The second kind of broad empathy I considered concerns, to quote Heal again, '[arriving] at judgements about others' thoughts, feelings, and so on from knowledge of their placement in the environment or bodily behaviour' (Heal 1996b: 45). When considering this second form of broad empathy, we looked at the distinction between 'empathetic perspective-shifting' and 'in-his-shoes perspective-shifting'. In the first, we imagine what it is like to be the target and take on their perspective and in the second we do not imagine what it is like to be the target, but imagine what it is like to 'be in their shoes'. We then distinguished between 'ambitious' and 'unambitious' versions of the latter. In the ambitious form, we imagine having the target's dispositions and desires, and in the unambitious form we do not; we simply imagine ourselves in the target's situation, and correct for what we know about them subsequently. I favoured unambitious in-his-shoes perspective-shifting as the most viable account of this second form of broad empathy.

Narrow empathy is a genus of the same species as this second form of broad empathy. Unlike the first form, it is not a matter of sharing contents so as to replicate a line of thought. Instead, it involves using our 'knowledge of their placement in the environment or bodily behaviour' to imagine what it is like for the target so as to bring about the same emotion, or an appropriately related emotion, to that felt by the target. Above, I argued that narrow empathy could be deliberate or involuntary. That gives us one axis for dividing various instance of narrow empathy. The other axis is between narrow empathy employed epistemically and narrow empathy employed for the sake of what I earlier called (following Joel Smith) 'transparent fellow-feeling'. This gives us four sorts of case: deliberate narrow empathy for epistemic reasons, involuntary narrow empathy for epistemic reasons, deliberate narrow empathy for reasons of transparent fellow-feeling and involuntary narrow empathy for reasons of transparent fellow-feeling. I shall begin by considering narrow empathy used for epistemic reasons.

Adam Smith, to repeat a quote from chapter 1, provides an instance of using narrow empathy (or 'sympathy', in his terms) in this way:

> By the imagination we place ourselves in [the other's] situation, we conceive of ourselves enduring all the same torments, we enter as it were into his body, and become in some measure the same person with him, and thence form some idea of his sensations, and even feel something which, though weaker in degree, is not altogether unlike them. (Smith 2002: 12)

Earlier, we examined an argument from Joel Smith: that we do not know how it feels to be in a certain mental state unless we are in some version of that state ourselves. Adam Smith seems to be making a stronger form of that claim: that we can only 'form some idea' of the target's sensations if we are in some version of that state ourselves. The reasons Adam Smith gives for holding this view are not compelling. He thinks that 'as we have no immediate experience of what other men feel, we can form no idea of the manner in which they are affected' (Smith 2002: 11). However, as Joel Smith himself points out, the idea that our only grounds for being able to judge *what* someone is feeling is a direct acquaintance with that feeling (or a mirror of that feeling in our own minds) is untenable. As we saw when examining Goldman's views, it might be that those unable to experience certain feelings are unable to detect (or have difficulty in detecting) that emotion in others' facial expressions. However, that is some way from the claim that, generally, attributing an emotion requires either, impossibly, a direct acquaintance with that emotion in the mind of the other or an acquaintance with its shadow in our own mind. There are many ways in which we can tell what a person is feeling, whether by observing their behaviour or (more simply) listening to what they say.

Even if Adam Smith's philosophy of mind is outdated, there is something to be said for our learning about others by imagining ourselves in their situation. The quotation from Smith above suggests deliberate behaviour: we 'place ourselves' in the other's situation. The deliberate exercise of narrow empathy for the purposes of finding out about others is most apparent when we are puzzled by another's reaction, or when we are consciously trying to broaden our understanding of the world. That is, there are occasions when we deliberately set out to imagine the world from a perspective somewhat distant from our own in an attempt to gain insight into the emotions (or motivations) experienced by someone who has that perspective. Consider an example of a world view that is likely to be very different from that held by any reader of this book: that of someone who appears to be living a satisfactory life who becomes a suicide bomber. Our motivation for attempting to empathize with such a person might be that one finds their actions incomprehensible and feels the need to try to make sense of those actions. As this is a case in which we are given the action and are attempting to find the motivation, it will be a case of 'generate and test' narrow empathy. It will also be a case in which we attempt not to make sense of some particular individual (although that is also possible) but of a type of person. One might, in a cool hour, attempt to imagine what it is like to be such a person. That is, one would need to acquire information about such a person's situation, and make various assumptions about their character. One would then imagine oneself in such a situation, factoring in what one has gathered about such a person's character and beliefs. These would be factors such as believing that their religion was not held with respect, that existing belief systems had no place for them, that those with whom they identified were deliberately and systematically oppressed, that violent acts against unbelievers were not only permitted but (in some circumstances) obligatory, that such acts would be rewarded in the afterlife, that alternatives that were on offer for them were not particularly attractive, and so on and so forth. If one vividly imagines it, one could find (perhaps even to one's surprise) a sense of anger or bitterness creeping into the imaginative project. This could provide grounds for making the judgement about what might drive suicide bombers. One could even, along with Kendall Walton and Joel Smith, come to believe that suicide bombers were motivated by *this*, where this is what one feels as a result of one's imaginative endeavours.

Of course, there are dangers – both epistemic and moral – in claiming to know what it is like to be another person. Our conclusions could be completely wrong. We might believe that we know what the target is feeling when, in fact, the target is feeling nothing of the sort. For this reason, the claim to know how another person feels, especially another person whose world view is different from ours, needs to be treated with sensitivity. To claim that we 'know how it feels' when we do not is a good platform for creating resentment or perpetrating injustice. Such a claim is sometimes appropriately met with a blunt dismissal; that we do not know anything about how it feels to be such a person in such a situation. This point is consonant with some that I make in the next chapter; that we have reason to be suspicious of empathy as a means to forming moral judgements.

The example just considered is the deliberate use of narrow empathy for epistemic reasons. Many of the relevant dispositions of the suicide bomber, such as a sense of resentment and an unquestioning acceptance of religious belief, will be part of the background of their deliberations. Many who attempt to imagine what it is like to be a suicide bomber will not share these dispositions. Such people will, in attempting to empathize, encounter the same problem we encountered in chapter 3. That is, in attempting to inhabit the bomber's perspective, those dispositions will not be part of the background of their deliberations but will be part of their deliberate attempt to re-create that perspective. Thus, there are limits to the ability to inhabit the perspectives of those who are different from us. Hence, the only option is unambitious in-his-shoes perspective-taking; we attempt to imagine what it would be like for us and then try to correct given what we know about the other's situation and character. That is, the deliberate use of narrow empathy for epistemic purposes goes along with unambitious in-his-shoes perspective-taking.

Can narrow empathy function epistemically when it is non-deliberate? In chapter 4, I discussed Goldman's claims that our own mirroring responses to others play a part in detecting what others feel. Such automatic affective reactions do not involve imagining what it is like to be the other or feeling what the other feels (except, at most, in a sub-personal sense); rather, they are part of the mechanism of 'reading' others. They belong to low-level simulation rather than to narrow empathy. However, I do think that there are cases in which narrow empathy is both non-deliberate and functions epistemically. I shall return to such cases when I discuss whether narrow empathy can acquaint us with emotions with which we were previously unfamiliar towards the end of this chapter.

Although Adam Smith thought narrow empathy could be used epistemically, he also, as we have seen, thought it had a quite different function:

> What are the pangs of a mother, when she hears the moanings of her infant that during the agony of disease cannot express what it feels? In her idea of what it suffers, she joins, to its real helplessness, her own consciousness of that helplessness, and her own terrors for the unknown consequences of its disorder; and out of all of these forms, for her own sorrow, the most complete image of misery and distress. (Smith 2002: 15)

It is clear from what Smith says here that the mother is not using narrow empathy as a way of finding out what her child is feeling. She knows very well what it is feeling; rather she has 'transparent fellow-feeling' with her child. When a friend describes his wretchedness at his ongoing divorce we imagine what it is like from his perspective. We do not do this in order to find out what he feels (at least, not usually, although I am not ruling it out); we do this to have transparent fellow-feeling with him – as the expression has it, 'we feel his pain'.

I said earlier that narrow empathy could be divided along two axes: between it functioning epistemically and it functioning for the sake of transparent fellow-feeling, and between it being deliberate and it being not deliberate. I considered deliberate epistemic uses of narrow empathy above and issued a promissory note to consider non-deliberate uses below. What of transparent fellow-feeling? Does this have deliberate and non-deliberate manifestations?

There is something odd about the deliberate exercise of narrow empathy for the sake of transparent fellow-feeling. It would be much like sympathy being deliberate; if the sympathy one feels for the target is under one's voluntary control, one might wonder whether it is properly sympathy at all. That is, either one has the disposition which will manifest itself in narrow empathy or one does not. If one has to deliberately inculcate narrow empathy, that is rather like feigning having the disposition rather than exercising it. There will be complicated situations (some of which we will discuss below) where one might believe one ought to empathize when one is not empathizing. In such a circumstance, one might try to empathize. However, that is not an instance of the deliberate exercise of narrow empathy for the sake of transparent fellow-feeling; rather, it is an instance of trying to get oneself into a position in which one is able to exercise empathy for the sake of transparent fellow-feeling non-deliberately.

The standard case of narrow empathy for the sake of transparent fellow-feeling is that it is not deliberate. We find ourselves, without willing it to be so, adopting the perspective of the target and feeling along with them. For this to truly be an instance of narrow empathy, my adopting the perspective of the target will need to factor in my beliefs about their situation and character. I argued above that even when we imagine involuntarily we are able to recruit our background beliefs into the imagined scenario. Hence, recruiting beliefs about a target's situation and character does not represent a problem in principle. However, as the process is involuntary, it cannot be an exercise of unambitious in-his-shoes perspective-taking, as unambitious in-his-shoes perspective-taking is under the control of the will. That is, unambitious in-his-shoes perspective-taking involves us imagining what it is like for us in a certain situation, and then deliberately correcting for what we believe about the target's situation and character. In instances of narrow empathy that are not deliberate this is not possible.

The reason for suggesting that we use unambitious in-his-shoes perspective-taking was the difficulty of making sense of the alternatives. We cannot adopt the perspective of a modest person if we are not modest. Modesty for them will be in the background of their deliberations; if it features at all for us, it would be consciously guiding our thoughts. Hence, the pay-off of not being able to use unambitious in-his-shoes perspective-taking is that instances of narrow empathy that are not deliberate are rather rough-and-ready. We are not able to make the fine adjustments in the light of what we believe about the target's situation and character. Rather, we imagine the world from something like the perspective of the target, factoring in something like their situation and character. As a consequence, the same caveats about claiming to 'know what it is like' to be the other person apply at least as much here as they did earlier when we considered the deliberate epistemic use of narrow empathy. It is as well to be cautious about claiming that what we are imagining is accurate; that we really are feeling what the target of our empathy is feeling.

I shall return to the issue of the reliability of narrow empathy below. Before that, however, I shall consider another intriguing question. Sometimes what we imagine (factoring information about a person's situation and character) is sufficient to generate an emotion and at other times it is not. Whether we are motivated to empathize narrowly for a target for epistemic reasons or for the sake of transparent fellow-feeling (or, as Joel Smith would argue, both), sometimes we are not successful. Despite our best efforts, we do not manage to generate any relevant emotion. Why is our imagination sometimes causally potent, and sometimes not? There is no reason to think that there is a simple answer to this question; the reasons are almost certainly many and various. I will consider three.

The first is that the onset of the feeling might be prevented by other facts about *our* mental state. We might be depressed, tired or simply moody. Even this embraces a number of different possibilities. First, it might be that the usual connections in our mental machinery are not operating. Delightful things do not delight us, upsetting things do not upset us and imaginative projects that would usually result in feelings do not result in feelings. To quote Coleridge on things that usually prompt a response from us, 'we see, not feel, how beautiful they are'.[2] The second is that we might not be able to face experiencing the negative emotion that would be aroused in us (that is, if the target is feeling a negative emotion). We empathize with the target, but the emotion generated – even if it is an emotion felt not for ourselves, but along with the target – is one that we are loath to experience. This is related to the third possibility; that empathizing would lead to personal distress. Although related to the ordinary language usage, 'personal distress' is a technical term in the philosophy and psychology of emotions. In a case of personal distress we feel an emotion as a result of believing that something bad has happened to the target, or believing or perceiving that the target feels that emotion, or adopting the perspective of the target who feels that emotion (Maibom 2014: 3). It differs from empathy in that the emotion is felt for oneself. It is not only that I feel sad with you that your dog has died, but that your being sad at your dog dying has made me feel sad for myself. As noted before, mental states do not generally arrive in an orderly fashion, one at a time. We usually experience a cluster of them together, and empathy is likely to shade into, or be experienced with, personal distress. Inasmuch as we all have reason to avoid personal distress, we have that reason to avoid empathy. Of course, this may not be an overriding reason; our motivation to feel empathy may well override our motivation to avoid personal distress.

The second reason why our imaginative project might not result in our feeling an emotion is, as Hume pointed out, that we might not feel any connection with the target.

> The stronger is the relation betwixt ourselves and any object, the more easily does the imagination make the transition, and convey to the related idea the vivacity of the conception, with which we always form the idea of our own person. Nor is resemblance the only relation, which has this effect, but receives new force from other relations, that may accompany it. The sentiments of others have little influence, when far remov'd from us, and require the relation of contiguity to make them communicate themselves entirely. The relations of blood, being a species of causation, may sometimes contribute to the same effect; as also acquaintance, which operated in the same manner with education and custom. (Hume 1739–40: I.ii.xi)

All things being equal, we are more likely to feel empathy for those close to us, our family and friends, than for those far away. The point is that we would be perfectly able to feel empathy for these people were the right relations (of kinship and so on) in place. We are not suffering from a lack of knowledge of their situation or character; it is rather that we are not motivated to care enough to empathize. As Neville Chamberlain remarked, it is not clear we should care about 'a quarrel in a far away country between people of whom we know nothing' (Chamberlain 1938). There is the possibility that the gap could be bridged, although when it comes to enumerating the ways in which this might happen, even Hume struggles. It could be by relations of resemblance, contiguity, kinship, cultural ties, and so on and so forth. Indeed, what does bridge the gap is unpredictable and often surprising. Images from far-away countries are constantly brought to our attention via the internet or the television news. We can be bombarded with images of destruction and horror, and yet remain largely unmoved. However, whole populations can be moved from indifference to intense empathy when a report focuses on the suffering of a particular person (in particular, an image of the suffering of a particular person), or some state of affairs with which it is easy to feel a kinship such as the death of a child.

The third reason why our imaginative project might not result in our feeling an emotion is a variety of the second. There might be something about the target that inhibits our feeling for them. This is supported by a study by Jean Decety and colleagues:

> Behavioural results showed that participants were significantly more sensitive to the pain of targets who were not responsible for their stigmatized condition (people who contracted AIDS as a result of blood transfusion) than either controls (healthy individuals) or targets who were held responsible for their condition (those who contracted AIDS through illegal drug use). In addition, participants expressed more empathy and personal distress in response to the pain of people who were not responsible for their stigmatized condition as compared with controls. Importantly, the differences between reactions to healthy controls and targets that were held responsible for their condition depended on individual differences in attributions of blame. The more participants blamed AIDS drug use targets for their condition, the less pain and empathy they reported when viewing their distress (compared with controls). (Decety et al. 2010: 994)

Our beliefs about the target's responsibility for his or her condition, or, more generally, whether or not he or she deserves to be in that condition, affects our levels of empathy (and, presumably, sympathy). Our beliefs about the target can also interact with our empathy in more subtle ways. In her book *The Empathy Exams*, Leslie Jamison tells of her experiences with the Morgellons community in the United States. Morgellons is a condition in which people believe themselves to be infested with parasites that live under the skin. Although opinion differs, it is generally believed that those suffering are delusional; that is, there are no such parasites. However, the suffering is genuine – compounded with the frustrations of not being believed. This complicates imagining what it is like to be a person in such a situation and with such a character. We imagine the world as viewed by someone who not only believes something we do not believe but where that belief will not be one we can understand a person having. By its nature, a delusion is not something those who do not have the delusion can share. Even if we can imagine what it is like from the perspective of a sufferer, it might not be clear what attitude to take to the resulting empathetic emotion (if any). As Jamison says, 'Is it wrong to call it empathy when you trust the fact of suffering, but not the source? How do I inhabit someone's pain without inhabiting their particular understanding of pain?' (Jamison 2014: ch. 2). Our attitudes to people's situation and our attitudes to their character will affect our empathy with them to the extent, says Jamison, that we might wonder whether this is properly called 'empathy'.

I have discussed only three limits to empathy, where our imaginative endeavours do not result in our feeling an emotion or result in an emotion to which our attitude is ambivalent. Even if our efforts at empathy do result in an emotion, the question arises as to whether that really is the emotion the target is feeling, or even whether it is something akin to the emotion the target is feeling. Once we experience an emotion as a result of imagining what it is like for the target, having factored in information about the target's situation and character, how certain can we be that the target is feeling that (or some appropriately related) emotion? For the remainder of this chapter I will examine some of the ways in which narrow empathy might be unreliable. There are many ways in which the attempt to empathize can go wrong. First, we could get the situation wrong or mistake the character of the target. Second, even if we got those right, they might be something beyond what we can imagine accurately – or even imagine. Third, the imagination is limited; there will be aspects of a face-to-face situation which it is impossible to simulate. Finally, there are some mental states that are impossible to simulate. Once again, the relevance of some of these considerations will only become fully apparent in the next chapter.

It is difficult to be so appraised of someone's situation and character that, no matter what the circumstances, their actions would never surprise you. We rarely know the details of people's lives, and few people if any are open about all of their dispositions, preferences and desires. Hence, an attempt at empathy might be flawed from the start. I have already mentioned this above, both with respect to deliberate attempts at narrow empathy and with our involuntarily feeling along with others. No matter how careful we are in our attempts to empathize, we could simply be wrong about the target's situation and character. We take on the perspective of someone whose partner has just died; in doing so, we imagine what it is like for someone suddenly deprived of the person who was most significant to them, of financial security and of their ambitions for the future. Unbeknownst to us, however, the target has long since ceased to love their partner and, furthermore, is due a massive insurance payout. The emotions we generate within ourselves revolve around loss and distress; the emotions the target is feeling revolve around relief and excitement, and – like Noël Coward's Mrs Wentworth-Brewster – a keen anticipation of a new life on Capri. Although problematic, the absence of true beliefs about situation and character does not raise any interesting philosophical problems specifically about empathy. Absence of true beliefs will hamper us in many of our projects, empathy included. All we can do is to work to ensure that we are as well informed as we can be.

The more interesting issue is whether, even if our grasp of the target's situation and character were accurate, we would always be able to imagine the world from their perspective. Peter Goldie neatly summarizes the problem:

> Speaking for myself, I do not find it difficult to empathize with my friend David who has been present at a rugby match which I have been watching on television. We both enjoy the sport, and we both support the same side. Here I will be able with considerable success centrally to imagine his emotions as he watches the game, and later as he makes his way back to the car park. When I turn to trying to empathize with the devout Mary Queen of Scots as she goes to her execution at Fotheringay on 8 February 1587, I fail completely, and would, I suspect, continue to fail however much I know about her and about what happened on that day. (Goldie 2000: 203)

Above I quoted Hume making the point that, even in circumstances in which empathy was possible, we might nonetheless fail as we lack the motivation because of an absence of a 'relation betwixt ourselves and any object'. In this case, Goldie does not lack the motivation to feel empathy for Mary Queen of Scots, and he also has the requisite information about her situation and character, and yet still fails. I said above, when considering suicide bombers, that we can attempt to imagine the world from perspectives that are distant from our own. What Goldie's example illustrates is that we will not always be successful. The gap between Goldie and Mary Queen of Scots was, he found, simply too wide. Goldie might have chosen that example because it is particularly difficult to imagine the state of mind that resulted in Mary's behaviour on the scaffold. She behaved in a fearless, dignified, even courtly, fashion. The task is to imagine what it was like to be in her situation (to be walking to one's death, which one did not think deserved) given her character (that of a devout Catholic). One knows her behaviour, so the task is to simulate the state of mind that could make such behaviour intelligible. Clearly, whatever Goldie came up with as going through the mind of someone walking to their death, with such a character, was not such as to render her behaviour intelligible. Our failure to imagine someone in a very different situation or with a very different character is not inevitable – as we saw in the case of suicide bombers. Goldie himself speculates that Antonia Fraser, the Catholic historian, might well succeed in the endeavour to imagine what it was like to be Mary Queen of Scots on that occasion. There will be a continuum here; we will be more or less successful in empathizing with other people. Sometimes we might be confident enough to say that we know 'exactly what someone is feeling'. At other times it would be as well to be more circumspect, and at yet further times as well to admit that, in Goldie's words, 'we fail completely'. The problem, and hence why this is an issue of the reliability of empathy, is that it might not be obvious to us which of these positions we are in. Hence, we might think we are more successful than in fact we are in empathizing with others. For an extended reflection on this kind of case, which uses it to cast doubt on contemporary approaches to empathy, see McFee (2011).

A second source of doubt as to the reliability of narrow empathy concerns whether the imagined inputs to our mental machinery have the same causal ramifications as the actual inputs in the target's mental machinery. At first sight, it seems that this should not be a problem. After all, in empathy I attempt to imagine the target's situation and character. The target is such that a string of beliefs and desires are being input into their mental machinery, the wheels are going round and the output is some feeling or emotion. In taking their perspective, I am feeding equivalents of their beliefs and desires into my mental machinery, and, given that my machinery is roughly the same as theirs, the same wheels will go round in the same way and produce an imagined version of the same (or some appropriately related) feeling or emotion. By empathizing with them I can produce tokens of the same (or some appropriately related) feeling or emotion.

Does the pattern of causation of the imagined inputs match that of beliefs? It is tempting to say no; that beliefs link to motivation and action, and imagined inputs do not. If I believe my dog is hungry, I will be motivated to feed it. If I simply imagine my dog is hungry, then I will not. However, that need not be a problem. The empathizer notes the feeling or emotion, and possibly the motivation to action, but does not act. To put the point in functionalist terms, this all happens in my 'possible world box', and the possible world box lacks the required connections to action.

Granting that the imagined inputs lack some of the causal powers of beliefs, in particular, that they lack a link to motivation and action, raises the question of whether imagined inputs might lack other causal powers. If I confront some difficult problem – for example, I have locked my keys in the house and need to pick up my wife from the airport – my mind races; I run through a range of options that might not usually occur to me. It might simply be that I need to believe I am locked out when I urgently need not to be to reach some of these options. We cannot assume, in advance, that imagining I am in this situation will do the work.

Let us explore this in more detail. It is tempting to think that if I vividly imagine, that is, really vividly imagine, I will be able to secure all the right links. However, we cannot assume that this is true; there is no reason to think that a phenomenological property – how brightly the thought shines in my imagination – corresponds to that thought's causal efficacy with respect to the rest of my mental machinery. It might be that beliefs have causal powers that imagined inputs, no matter how vividly held, cannot have. Consider a situation which, even if it is not one that I have experienced myself, is part of my world in the sense that it has happened to many people that I know: the first time one sees one's first child. I might try to empathize with a friend, whose character is familiar to me, so as to experience what he or she experienced in such a situation. It might be that no matter how vividly I attempt to imagine what it is like for him or her I will always fail. The imagined state just will not have the right links to the right emotions; I simply cannot raise the right kind of nurturing feelings. Here is another example. Consider being a witness to an incident involving a motorcycle. You see your friend come round the corner on their bike, swerve to avoid a cat, and head straight towards an oncoming car. He or she desperately tries to brake, while at the same time heading towards the small gap between the car and the side of the road. You vividly occupy your friend's perspective; your heart is in your mouth, you are filled with panic as all flashes before you. However, afterwards, when you discuss it, your friend reports (as often is reported by people who have faced extreme danger) that they felt no panic at all; their minds were completely clear, and everything seemed to be moving slowly; slowly enough for them to make decisions. Presumably what is happening here is that the belief has caused physiological and psychological changes (a release of adrenalin, a clarity of thought) that have evolved to enable a person to cope better in such situations. Imaginatively putting oneself in his or her situation simply does not have these effects, and hence the empathizer arrives at the wrong conclusion about what the target felt.

Furthermore, there are other aspects of confrontations that simply cannot be captured in the imagination. Let us consider an example. Here is an excerpt from a letter by Charlotte Brontë in which she describes receiving a proposal of marriage from her father's curate, a Mr Nicholls:

As usual – Mr N sat with Papa till between eight and nine o'clock. I then heard him open the parlour door as if going. I expected the clash of the front door – He stopped in the passage: he tapped: like lightning it flashed on me what was coming. He entered – he stood before me. What his words were – you can guess his manner – you can hardly realise – nor can I forget it – Shaking from head to foot, looking deadly pale, speaking low, vehemently yet with difficulty – he made me for the first time feel what it costs a man to declare affection where he doubts response. The spectacle of one ordinarily so statue-like – thus trembling, stirred, and overcome gave me a kind of strange shock. He spoke of suffering he had borne for months – of sufferings he could endure no longer – and craved leave for some hope. (Barker 2006: 377)

In reading this passage one wants, as Charlotte Brontë does, to empathize with Mr Nicholls. We have, from Brontë's other letters, a grasp of his character and, unless one is particularly fortunate, one can have a grasp of his situation. Perhaps with some further work (a visit to Haworth Parsonage would help) one is able to occupy his perspective. However, in addition to some of the other reasons given for being sceptical of the power of empathy to deliver the right feeling or emotion, there are two further problems.

The first is that there are many things about Mr Nicholls's situation that are simply out of reach of the imagination. It is familiar to those in the first throes of passion that certain things – the way the person holds their head, the way they set their mouth, the smell of their hair – can be intoxicating. Not only is there no way for us to know whether factors such as this are contributing to Mr Nicholls's agitation but, even if we did know about them, we could not duplicate them in our imagination. The second is that the state we are attempting to replicate has Charlotte Brontë as its object; all Mr Nicholls's attention is directed towards *her* in her full particularity. This raises one of the issues we considered in looking at Maibom's definition of 'affective empathy'. We do not feel what Mr Nicholls is feeling in that his feeling, unlike ours, is focused on Charlotte Brontë and bound up with an array of attitudes towards her to which we do not have access. It is always possible that we could give up trying to be empathetic, and simply feel sympathy for the man. In that case, which is of course also possible, what we feel would not have the complex overlap with what he feels that I have described. In this simpler case, we might simply feel something like compassion or pity for Mr Nicholls.

Shifting to feeling sympathy, however, is not the only option. Modulo what was said above about non-rational influences, and on whether our imagined inputs would have causal powers akin to Mr Nicholls's actual inputs, it is possible that our attempts at empathy could result in our coming to feel something like what it was that he felt. We are unlikely to capture exactly what it was like for him, but, in the sense specified earlier, we could capture something akin to what it was like, without Charlotte Brontë, but rather something more baldly specified and indeterminate, as our emotion's object. We should not set the bar so high as to make empathy impossible, but the pay-off is that we should not be over-ambitious in what we claim on its behalf.

The question of whether imagined inputs can have the same causal effects as beliefs is sharpened when we consider whether narrow empathy could be the route to our becoming acquainted with emotions we have never previously encountered. Although I think something like this can happen, there are at least two reasons to be cautious. The first is that, for adults at least, it is not clear that there are feelings or emotions that people have never previously encountered. As I have said, feelings and emotions are complex states; they have cognitive elements, phenomenological elements, physiological elements, and generally come with some hedonic tone – either positive or negative. Hence, whatever the candidate for an entirely novel feeling or emotion, we are bound to have experienced something a little like it before. Trying to imagine what things are like for some person might involve imagining an emotion that is deeper than, or more desperate than, any we have felt before. However, it is unlikely to be an emotion that previously was entirely unfamiliar to us.

In attempting to counter this view, someone might argue that there are well-known instances of feelings or emotions that are entirely novel. We encountered one of these in the discussion above; the feeling one gets on first seeing one's first child. Another candidate would be what one feels when one first falls in love. Folk wisdom suggests that these require first-hand acquaintance; they are the kinds of emotion of which people say 'You don't know what it is like until it happens to you'. It is largely an empirical question as to whether we could be introduced to such feelings or emotions through empathy, but let us accept the folk wisdom, at least provisionally. That is, accept that there are some emotions beyond the reach of mere imaginative endeavour; that in order to narrowly empathize with someone who is experiencing such an emotion, one must have already experienced it oneself. This raises the issue of the relation between empathy and memory.

Let us return to the story of Mr Crane and Mr Tees; the two people who missed their planes, the first by twenty-five minutes and the second by five minutes. I said above that 'The imaginative process leading to this judgement is, it seems fair to assume, that the subjects imagine what things are like from each of Mr Crane and Mr Tees's perspectives and find occupying the latter perspective involves more upset.' Even if this is right, the claim is compatible with two different processes happening in our minds. In the first process we input the relevant make-beliefs, the wheels turn round, and we end up, in imagination, feeling less upset if we make-believe we missed the plane by twenty-five minutes than we do if we make-believe we missed the plane by five minutes. The second process also involves inputting the relevant make-beliefs. However, instead of the wheels going round, these inputs activate a memory trace of all those times when we have missed catching something, and we recall that we were less upset in those cases where we missed that thing by a comfortable margin than we were if we missed it by only a whisker.

We would not be able to tell, by introspection, which process was operating; there is nothing in our experiences which would tell us whether or not memory traces were operative. Both processes involve an experiential element; we would, in imagination, feel the upset. That is, when memory traces are activated, we would not remember *that* we had been upset, we would remember *being upset*. Kendall Walton, who introduced this idea, speculates that 'memory traces of some sort play an important role in just about all imaginative experiments of the kind we are considering and that there are few if any *pure* instances of mental (process) simulation' (Walton 1999: 137). Walton's view seems right, and further reflection seems to reinforce his point. It is likely that the gap between ourselves and the targets with whom we are attempting to empathize will be smaller if we have been in the target's situation ourselves than it would be if we had not been in that situation. Consider a scenario in which someone is reporting a conversation in which their doctor has told them that they have cancer. You take their perspective; you can visualize the doctor's serious face, and hear the fateful words. If you have been in that situation yourself there is less work for you to do; your imaginative effort need not be so great. You can simply recruit the memory traces of how you felt when you were told, and use that to prompt, in imagination, what they felt. You empathize; you are grasping the person's situation and their character, and you are feeling along with them. Nonetheless, you achieve this not only by inputting imaginative analogues of their mental states, but by doing this alongside remembering what it was like for you when you were in that situation. Indeed, if memory traces were not involved, it would be difficult to explain the general phenomenon that the gap between empathizer and target is smaller if the empathizer has had the same (or similar) experience to that of the target. Hence, another limitation to empathy is whether the situation is one that is new to the empathizer, or whether it is one that they have encountered before.

I see no reason, however, to think that it is impossible for someone, in some sense, to learn what a certain emotional experience is like through empathy. Empathizing with someone face-to-face is perhaps more unusual than imagining what it is like to be someone on the basis of information received indirectly. However, as we know, it does happen. Suppose that a close friend is pouring their heart out about their ongoing divorce. Furthermore, suppose they are someone who is not very psychologically different from you, in that you broadly share dispositions, hopes and fears. As they relate the various dramatic events, their face reveals their feelings. In such a circumstance, one would have an abundance of information that one could use as input, together with an abundance of information as to the actual output. This would not principally be a case of empathizing to find out what they are feeling; the aim would be to achieve transparent fellow-feeling. In the attempt at transparent fellow-feeling you might venture into areas of the emotional spectrum with which you had not previously been acquainted. It is not only during encounters with others who are actually feeling emotions that this might happen. It may well be that one function of drama is to introduce audiences to areas of the emotional spectrum with which they are unfamiliar. Once again, audiences do not lack information as to what to use as input, and they are guided by what they see in front of them as to the appropriate output. Imagining what it is like for the various characters on the stage can be an emotionally harrowing experience; we can, for example, capture something of what it would be like to be in King Lear's situation, without having actually to endure those experiences. However, this is taking us into the topic of chapter 8.

The tenor of my discussion has been slightly sceptical about narrow empathy. I do not doubt that it occurs. We can consciously work to understand someone's situation and character, imagine ourselves into their perspective and feel what they feel. We can also be prompted involuntarily to take on someone's perspective in imagination and feel what they feel. However, we should be modest in the claims we make on its behalf. Partly because we are trying to replicate what it is like to be in some emotional state, there are many ways in which attempts at empathy can fail. We might lack information about the target's situation or we might lack a grasp of what, in their situation, is salient to them. We might misconstrue their character, or it might simply be that our imagined inputs do not have the same causal ramifications in our mental economy as their actual inputs have in theirs. Emotional states are notoriously sensitive to details, and a salient detail from the target's perspective might simply be something that either cannot or does not register from the empathizer's perspective.

7
Empathy and Ethics

In his book, *Empathy: A Handbook for Revolution*, Roman Krznaric makes great claims for the capacity of empathy to change our world for the better:

> When a critical mass of people join together to make the imaginative leap into the lives of others, empathy has the power to alter the contours of history. For each and every one of us, the culmination of our empathic journeys is to help create these waves of collective empathy that can play a part in tackling the great problems of our age, from poverty and inequality to armed violence and environmental collapse. (Krznaric 2014: no pagination)

Indeed, the link between empathy and ethics might seem obvious enough to ground the thought that anyone who denies there is such a link is confused about what 'empathy' means. Certainly, there is a use of 'empathy' in which the link with ethical concern seems analytic. We praise friends or therapists for being empathetic, and various sorts of professionals are tested on whether they display this trait. Leslie Jamison describes playing the role of a patient as part of the training for hospital doctors. As such, she is required to fill in a checklist for how the trainees perform against various measures.

Checklist item 31 is generally acknowledged as the most important category: 'Voiced empathy for my situation/problem.' We are instructed about the importance of the first word, *voiced*. It is not enough for someone to have a sympathetic manner or use a caring tone. The students have to say the right words to get credit for compassion. (Jamison 2014: ch. 1)

Jamison worries, rightly, as to whether verbalizing one's compassion is the crucial issue, as opposed to simply displaying it – indeed, how, for the patient, the latter is often preferable to the former. However, whether merely verbalized or displayed through behaviour, she assumes there to be a link between empathy and concern for the individual patient. Empathy is manifested in 'a sympathetic manner' or 'caring tone', and she equates empathy with compassion.

Despite the foregoing, both the link between empathy and compassion and the link between compassion and ethics turn out to be problematic. So far in this book I have used two definitions of 'empathy': the broad definition (which broadly equates to 'simulation') and the narrow definition (otherwise known as 'affective empathy'). I argued that broad empathy is primarily used to find out what is going on in the head of another person (the 'target'), and narrow empathy is sometimes used for this purpose, and sometimes to exhibit 'transparent fellow-feeling' with the target. Neither in the case of broad empathy nor in the case of narrow empathy is the connection with ethics obvious. That is, there seems to be a gap between knowing what someone thinks or knowing how they feel (or even feeling how they feel) and treating them in an ethically appropriate manner.

While it is true that philosophy has tended to focus on empathy as I have been discussing it, the use of 'empathy' that links it to compassion has not been entirely neglected. In a paper discussing the link between empathy and virtue, Heather Battaly gives the following definition (one of a number of different definitions that she lists):

Empathy is a process of caring, or sharing, or knowing, or some combination thereof...[This definition] is meant to capture the empathy of one's best friend or therapist, ordinarily construed. Best friends and therapists often *care* about the target for his own sake; their motivations are often altruistic. They often *share* the emotions (or other mental states) of the target, and they typically understand, *know*, and can predict the target's emotions, beliefs, and actions. (Battaly 2011: 278–9)

If this is what we mean by 'empathy', there will be a close link between empathy and, at least, compassion. Empathizing with someone is bound up with caring about them for their own sake as a matter of definition.

Whether or not this is what is generally meant by 'empathy', the definition combines two things: taking the perspective of another person and caring for that other person. As I said above, it is not obvious how these are related. Peter Goldie points out that the mental states we inculcate in ourselves as a result of taking the perspective of another person are compatible with a number of other attitudes to the target:

First, they are consistent with indifference: you can imagine the other's suffering, yet simply disregard it; or you might empathise with a person who has committed a terrible crime, yet feel no normative demands to help him, for you think he thoroughly deserves his punishment. Secondly, they are consistent with a response which is the *opposite* of sympathetic, involving *rejoicing* in the other's suffering, or even, like the subtle and imaginative inquisitor, exploiting your sensitivity of the other's feelings to help you exacerbate his suffering. And thirdly, they are consistent with motivations and actions aimed at alleviation of one's own suffering, rather than the other's. For example, one might turn away at the sight of blood, or turn off the television to avoid watching the reports of the latest famine; and if you gave money to the beggar, it would be to get him out of your sight, it being only an unintended side-effect of your action if this were also to alleviate his suffering. (Goldie 2000: 215)

We can use our knowledge of what is going on in the head of another for good or evil. It is not made clear in George Orwell's *1984* how O'Brien knows the content of Winston Smith's greatest fear. However, that he does know, and knows that Winston is terrified beyond measure, is compatible with him making use of that knowledge to deprive Winston of all that is left to him. There is no *conceptual* connection between taking the perspective of another person and caring for that person.

Even if there is not conceptual connection, however, there may well still be a causal connection. That is, human nature being what it is, being empathic towards another may result in taking a caring attitude to that other. Indeed, as mentioned in chapter 1, David Hume made this the foundation of his moral theory. This is not the place for an extended account of Hume on morality, but his work does nicely introduce two themes with which I will deal in this chapter.

The first is that empathy (or, in Hume's terms, sympathy) is foundational for morality. We can draw a crude contrast between two approaches to moral thought: the approach which holds that we arrive at our moral distinctions by the use of reason and what lies at the basis of our moral distinctions are reasons, and the approach which holds that we arrive at our moral distinctions by exercising our sentiments and that what lies at the basis of our moral distinctions are our sentiments. Hume is the champion of the latter approach.

The passage from Hume that I quoted in chapter 1 was from a section of the *Treatise* entitled 'Of the origin of the natural virtues and vices'. I shall quote it again, together with the passage that immediately follows it:

> We may begin with considering a-new the nature and force of sympathy. The minds of all men are similar in their feelings and operations, nor can any one be actuated by any affection, of which all others are not, in some degree, susceptible. As in strings wound up, the motion of one communicates itself to the rest; so all the affections readily pass from one person to another, and beget correspondent movements in every human creature. When I see the *effects* of passion in the voice and gesture of any person, my mind immediately passes from these effects to their causes, and forms such a lively idea of the passion, as is presently converted into the passion itself. In like manner, when I perceive the *causes* of any emotion, my mind is convey'd to the effects, and is actuated with a like emotion. Were I present to any of the more terrible operations of surgery, 'tis certain, that even before it begun, the preparation of the instruments, the laying of the bandages in order, the heating of the irons, with all the signs of anxiety and concern in the patient and assistants, wou'd have a great effect upon my mind, and excite the strongest sentiments of pity and

terror. No passion of another discovers itself immediately to the mind. We are only sensible of its causes or effects. From *these* we infer the passion: And consequently, *these* give rise to our sympathy. (Hume 1739–40: III.iii.i)

The principal concern of moral evaluation, for Hume, is the assessment of others and also of ourselves. We value people as exhibiting discretion, caution, enterprise, industry, assiduity, frugality, economy, good-sense, prudence, discernment, temperance, sobriety, patience, constancy, perseverance, forethought, considerateness, secrecy, order, insinuation, address, presence of mind, quickness of conception and facility of expression, to take the list Hume provides in the *Enquiries* (Hume 1902: VI.i (242–3)). However, in assessing others we face a problem. As Hume says, 'no passion of another discovers itself immediately to the mind'. The principal way in which we come to learn of these character traits in others is by observing their effects – in particular, the effects the exercise of these traits has on other people. We learn this by empathizing with those who are thus affected. If our empathizing results in a feeling of approbation, that is the moral sentiment of approval towards that trait or action, and we count it a virtue. If our empathizing results in disapprobation, that is the moral sentiment of disapproval towards that trait or action, and we count it a vice.

The same mechanism underpins our commitment to justice. Hume points out, quite rightly, that sometimes 'a single act of justice, consider'd in itself, may often be contrary to the public good' (Hume 1739–40: III.ii.ii). Such a realization might license the thought that it would be better for the public good if such 'single acts of justice' did not happen; if they could somehow be avoided. Thus, we might try to set up a system in which generally things happen justly, but on single occasions when doing the just thing would be 'contrary to the public good' we make an exception and allow single acts of injustice to occur. However, there are well-known problems with any such mixed system. There are the problems of working out which particular unjust acts we should allow. After all, unjust acts often benefit the person who acts; in such cases, it is easy for such a person to convince themselves that it would be better overall, and not just for themselves, if the act was allowed. There would also be the problem that justice would be unsystematic, unreliable and hence unpredictable. We would not know, of some anticipated action, whether it would happen or whether it would be counted an exception. It is only if justice is universal, and consistently applied, that it will benefit us overall. How is it that, given that justice is sometimes contrary to the public good, human beings come to support it? Once again, the answer is sympathy. We experience feelings of disapprobation when we observe people being treated unjustly, and this motivates us to be just and support their being treated justly even if it is opposed to the public (or our own) interest: '*Thus self-interest is the original motive to the* establishment *of justice: but a* sympathy *with public interest is the source of the moral approbation, which attends the virtue*' (Hume 1739–40: III.ii.ii).

Our empathy with those affected, and the resulting feelings of approbation and disapprobation, leave us in the right territory for morality. The fact that we are in the realm of feelings (or, in the parlance of the eighteenth century, the passions) connects morality with action. Feeling someone else's discomfort gives us a good reason to alleviate that discomfort (although, as we shall see, this is more complicated than it seems) in a way that merely believing that someone else is discomfited does not. For Hume, the passions are a necessary pre-condition for action: 'reason alone can never be a motive to any action or will' (Hume 1739–40: II.iii.ii). This makes prima facie sense, and, as we will see, is the starting point for a number of views as to the role of empathy in morality today. That is, it is easier to see how compassion, and subsequent caring behaviour, could begin in our actually feeling the hurt of the victim, rather than simply believing that the victim is hurt.

The second theme is raised by Hume himself as a putative problem for his view. The feelings engendered by empathy, as we know, vary greatly depending on how close we are to the target. Moral sentiments, however, are not supposed to be subject to such partiality.[1] Hence, empathy cannot be the grounds of the moral sentiments.

> When any quality, or character, has a tendency to the good of mankind, we are pleas'd with it, and approve of it; because it

presents the lively idea of pleasure; which idea affects us by sympathy, and is itself a kind of pleasure. But as this sympathy is very variable, it may be thought, that our sentiments of morals must admit of the same variations. We sympathise more with persons contiguous to us, than with persons remote from us: With our acquaintances, than with strangers: With our countrymen, than with foreigners. But notwithstanding this variation of our sympathy, we give the same approbation to the same moral qualities in China as in England. They appear equally virtuous, and recommend themselves equally to the esteem of a judicious spectator. The sympathy varies without a variation of our esteem. Our esteem, therefore, proceeds not from sympathy. (Hume 1739–40: III.iii.i)

One promised benefit of grounding morality in reason is that reason does not admit of the kind of variation Hume adduces. Reasons are general; if I have reason to think someone a vicious character who should be avoided, then, unless the circumstances are relevantly different, it will also be a reason for you to think that person a vicious character who should be avoided. That those affected by the person are close to me and not to you, or my countrymen rather than your countrymen, does not constitute a relevant difference. Having raised the issue, Hume goes on to argue that it is not a problem for the sentimentalist approach:

But to consider the case a-right, it has no force at all; and 'tis the easiest matter in the world to account for it. Our situation, with regard both to persons and things, is in continuous fluctuation; and a man, that lies at a little distance from us, may, in a little time, become a familiar acquaintance. Besides, every particular man has a peculiar position with regard to others; and 'tis impossible we cou'd ever converse together on any reasonable terms, were each of us to consider characters and persons, only as they appear from his peculiar point of view. In order, therefore, to prevent the continual contradictions, and arrive at a more stable judgement of things, we fix on some steady and general points of view; and always, in our thoughts, place ourselves in them, whatever may be our present situation. (Hume 1739–40: III.iii.i)

Hume elsewhere speaks of 'some common point of view, from which [people] might survey their object, and which might cause it to appear the same to all of them' (Hume 1739–40: III.iii.i). The form of the solution is fairly obvious, even if it takes some complicated working out to make it plausible.[2] We need to abstract from our particular relations with those affected, and from the contingencies that may or may not govern the full exercise of the trait. Roughly, we should take on the perspective of anyone, regardless of their situation or the character, who would be affected were the trait to be exercised. This, then, will require more work than the associationism Hume has relied on previously – that is, the painful awareness of the effects of the trait carrying us to the thought of the trait. In taking up 'the common point of view' we need to imagine ourselves into the position of those who would be thus affected, even if we are not contiguous with them.

What we get from Hume, then, are two thoughts: that empathy plays a key role in the generation of moral sentiments, and that those sentiments need to be 'corrected' so that our moral sentiments do not end up being viciously partial. As we shall see, these two points are still central to the modern debate.

The person who has done most to advance the debate over the link between empathy and caring behaviour is the psychologist Daniel C. Batson. For decades, Batson has been considering whether human behaviour is motivated by altruism or by egoism. He defends what he calls 'the empathyaltruism hypothesis': 'the claim that feeling empathic emotion for someone in need evokes altruistic motivation to relieve that need' (Batson et al. 2012: 419). It will help clarify the debate if we define some terms. Although Batson's definitions have varied in their detail over the course of his research, the basic structure of the account has remained constant.

By 'empathic concern', Batson means 'other-oriented emotion elicited by and congruent with the perceived welfare of the person in need'. This emotion 'is not a single, discrete emotion' but includes 'feelings of sympathy, compassion, softheartedness, tenderness, sorrow, sadness, upset, distress, concern, and grief' (Batson 2014: 41–2). He is not, in this definition, attempting to capture everything that anyone has ever meant by 'empathy'. Indeed, he distinguishes his definition from seven other definitions of the term, including various forms of perspective-taking and 'coming to feel as another feels' (Batson 2014: 42). Clearly, the definition with which he is working is related to those discussed above which draw a conceptual link between empathy and care and compassion.

As Batson's definition links empathy with care or compassion, one might wonder what the debate is about. If the link is present by definition then the empathy-altruism hypothesis would surely be true by definition: if someone feels care or compassion for someone else, that would surely prompt altruistic motivations (even if, for practical reasons, those motivations were thwarted). This, however, misconstrues the nature of Batson's project. To grasp the nature of that project, let us first assume that empathic concern does motivate compassionate behaviour. This still leaves the question of the *mechanism* underpinning that motivation. The problem Batson has in mind can be seen if we contrast two different accounts of human motivation. On the one side is the doctrine of psychological hedonism. This is the claim that all our motivations (including those to do good) are egotistical: to do with advancing our own welfare. On the other side is the claim that among our motivations can be found some that are altruistic: motivations focused on helping others for their own sake. Batson's primary concern is to discover whether our fundamental motivations, the forces which drive us, are egotistical or altruistic.

Although there are exceptions, it is generally true that those working in mainstream philosophy take the view that psychological hedonism is either trivial or false. The mainstream philosophical view is concerned with explaining actions by reference to propositional attitudes such as belief and desire. Thus, for mainstream philosophy, psychological hedonism could be construed in one of two ways. First, it could be construed as the claim that we desire the satisfaction of our desires. This is the trivial version, as that is simply part of what it is to have a desire. Alternatively, it could be construed as the claim that, ultimately, all desires are 'I-desires'; they have, as part of their content, some reference to the person who has the desire. In this case, the thesis is false as we have plenty of desires that make no reference to ourselves (Williams 1973b: 261). By contrast, Batson takes the notion of psychological hedonism seriously. He does not take it to be a thesis about the role of desires in explaining action, but rather a thesis about the brute psychological forces that govern our actions. To better understand this, we need to attend to the way in which he defines the terms he uses. By 'egoism', Batson means 'a motivational state with the ultimate goal of increasing one's own welfare' and by 'altruism' he means 'a motivational state with the ultimate goal of increasing another's welfare' (Batson 2014: 43). By 'motivational state', he means 'a goal directed psychological force within an organism' (Batson and Shaw 1991: 108).

Batson has a substantial enough conception of goal-directedness to restrict this to 'the higher mammals', but it is clearly nothing to do with propositional attitudes. Rather, it is a non-intentional, sub-personal state. If a person acts on a desire that is focused on someone else – a desire, for example, to increase the welfare of another – then, at an intentional level, that would count as altruistic. However, for Batson it is an open question as to whether it really is altruistic; the deep motivational state may well be egoistic. His question as to whether the empathy-altruism hypothesis is true is the question as to whether being empathetic makes a difference to the nature of our deep motivational states. That is, do people who are empathetic act on egoistic motivations or altruistic motivations? His methodology is to specify an exhaustive list of egoistic motivational states and then show, by psychological tests, that those who act out of feelings of empathy are not primarily motivated by these states.

> Three possible self-benefits of empathy-induced helping have been identified, producing three egoistic alternatives to the empathy-altruism hypothesis: (a) aversive arousal reduction – reducing the empathic concern caused by witnessing another in need; (b) punishment avoidance – avoiding empathy-specific material, social, and self-punishments; and (c) reward-seeking – gaining empathy specific material, social, and self-rewards. (Batson 2014: 44; see also Batson and Shaw 1991: 110–12)

The first of these motivations is the avoidance of personal distress: reducing the arousal of aversive states caused by witnessing another in need. In feeling empathy towards a person in need, you come to feel certain unpleasant feelings yourself and the actions you take to help that other person are motivated by an urge to alleviate these unpleasant feelings. The second possibility is that you are acting to avoid social sanctions: being blamed for not acting so as to alleviate the need of another. The third possibility is that you are acting to gain reward through the feeling of having alleviated the need of another; the warm glow that is consequent upon performing actions of that nature.

His conclusions are tentative:

> There are now more than 35 experiments designed to test the empathy-altruism hypothesis against one or more of the egoistic alternatives. Results of these experiments have consistently patterned as predicted by the empathy-altruism hypothesis and have failed to support any of the egoistic alternatives. To the best of my knowledge, there is no plausible egoistic explanation for the cumulative evidence from these experiments. This evidence has led me to conclude – tentatively – that the egoism-altruism hypothesis is true, that empathic concern produces altruistic motivation. Further, this altruistic motive can be surprisingly powerful. (Batson 2014: 44–5)

Clearly, Batson's definition of 'altruism' is a psychological term of art that cuts across definitions in philosophy and, for that matter, ordinary language. Much of what counts for Batson as egoistic will count for us as altruistic. Thus, insofar as the level of explanation with which we are concerned is that of beliefs and desires, Batson's conclusions will be of limited interest. This is not in itself a criticism; a science such as psychology will need technical terms. It is still an interesting result – consonant with Hume's thinking – that, no matter how far down in our psychologies we go, empathy tends to result in motivations to act that have no pay-off for the actor; that are directed solely to advancing the interests of the target for their own sake.

Even if Batson's conclusions are relatively unilluminating for the philosophical debate,[3] there are other psychologists who are prepared to venture consonant conclusions at the level of beliefs and desires. One of these is Martin Hoffman, who has been studying the link between empathy and what is called in the literature 'pro-social behaviour' for many years. His principal work is his book *Empathy and Moral Development* (Hoffman 2000). He has summed up his findings (at least with respect to moral motivation) in a later paper:

> The overwhelming evidence... is that most people, when they witness someone in distress, feel empathically distressed and motivated to help. Thus empathy has been found repeatedly to correlate positively with helping others in distress, even strangers, and negatively with aggression and manipulative behaviour. More important, experiments show that empathy arousal leads observers to help victims, and furthermore they are more quick to help the more intense their empathic distress and the more intense the victim's pain. Additionally, observers' empathic distress decreases more quickly and they feel better when they help than when they don't help and when despite their best efforts the victim's distress is not alleviated. (Hoffman 2011: 231)

There is much that could be said about Hoffman's work, what he means by 'empathy', what counts as a 'pro-social motive', and the relation between such motives and morality. However, I shall pass over this as most of the substantial points come out in the discussion below. Let us grant that empathy, on some plausible definition, contributes to actions aimed at increasing the welfare of others. That is, the first of the two links discussed at the beginning of this chapter is in place: there is some link, if only a contingent one, between feeling empathy and feeling compassion.

This leaves, then, the second of the two links: between feeling compassion (or exhibiting 'pro-social behaviour') and morality. With this established, we would have shown that empathy has a place as one of the building-blocks of morality. Here, perhaps surprisingly, matters are not that simple. Recently there has been a groundswell of opinion that seeks to counterpose empathy and the actions that result from empathy, and morality. In September 2014, Paul Bloom caused a storm by announcing in the pages of *The Boston Review* that he was 'against empathy': 'if you want to be good and do good, empathy is a poor guide'. His principal reason for holding this is the second of the lessons we took from Hume. That empathy is partial, and, if it is to be of any use to morality at all, needs to be 'corrected'. Bloom's case against empathy is forceful:

> Empathy is biased; we are more prone to feel empathy for attractive people and for those who look like us or share our ethnic or national background. And empathy is narrow; it connects us to particular individuals, real or imagined, but is insensitive to numerical differences and statistical data. As Mother Teresa put it, "If I look at the mass I will never act. If I look at the one, I will." Laboratory studies find that we really do care more about the one than about the mass, so long as we have personal information about the one.
>
> In light of these features, our public decisions will be fairer and more moral once we put empathy aside. Our policies are improved when we appreciate that a hundred deaths are worse than one, even if we know the name of the one, and when we acknowledge that the life of someone in a faraway country is worth as much as the life of a neighbor, even if our emotions pull us in a different direction. Without empathy, we are better able to grasp the importance of vaccinating children and responding to climate change. These acts impose costs on real people in the here and now for the sake of abstract future benefits, so tackling them may require overriding empathetic responses that favor the comfort and well being of individuals today. We can rethink humanitarian aid and the criminal justice system, choosing to draw on a reasoned, even counter-empathetic, analysis of moral obligation and likely consequences. (Bloom 2014)

The same point has been made by the former Archbishop of Canterbury, Rowan Williams, in the first of his Tanner lectures on Human Value entitled, appropriately enough, 'The Paradoxes of Empathy'.[4] Williams draws one of the examples he uses from his experience of visiting the Middle East (I have changed the example somewhat, but not in a way that changes the point). One can visit a Palestinian village which has been bombed by Israel and feel a great deal of empathy for the inhabitants. One can then visit those in Israel who have been injured, or had relatives killed, by Palestinian activists and feel a great deal of empathy for them. However, such feelings of empathy do nothing to sort out the morally appropriate action, let alone a just resolution to the conflict.

Taking empathy and morality to be closely aligned misses the fact that morality is a matter of relations within a culture, or across cultures. Even if we have a good understanding of who feels empathy for whom, and why, all the interesting moral and political questions still remain.

Jesse Prinz has attempted to spell out in detail the ways in which empathy and morality pull us in different directions. Prinz argues for the narrow thesis that empathy is not necessary for morality: 'empathy is not necessary for the capacities that make up basic moral competence: one can acquire moral virtues, make moral judgements, and act morally without empathy' (Prinz 2011: 213). The problems Prinz finds in the relation between empathy and morality are consonant with those that concerned Hume concerning the fact that sympathy (or empathy) is partial while morality at least aspires to being impartial. Prinz raises eight different issues that bring out the limitations of empathy as a basis for morality. I shall divide these into four broader headings.

First, in comparison with emotions such as outrage, 'empathy is not very motivating' (Prinz 2011: 225). Prinz is a Humean about morality, at least to the extent that he thinks moral judgements have their basis in our emotions. The issue is whether having empathy provide the emotion at the core of the judgement will be any more motivating than having some alternative source provide that emotion. Prinz argues persuasively that there is little reason to think that the former are more motivating; indeed, he cites empirical evidence to show that among children there is no correlation between empathy and pro-social behaviour, and only modest correlations in adults (Prinz 2011: 219).[5] Intuitively this makes sense; feelings of anger, disgust, guilt and shame are the kinds of feelings that motivate behaviour. It is not clear why emotions that stem from perspective-taking should, in general, be as motivating, let alone more motivating.

Second, 'empathy can be easily manipulated' (Prinz 2011: 226). Hoffman describes the many ways and means in which lawyers deliberately set out to get juries to empathize with their clients; indeed, he claims that doing so is taught in courtroom training manuals. Getting defendants to express emotion, appear vulnerable and so on increases the likelihood of acquittal or a lighter sentence (Hoffman 2011: 251–3).

Looked at from the other side, getting victims to express emotion, appear vulnerable and so on increases the likelihood of a harsher sentence. It is the latter fact that underpins the worries some have about the use of 'victim impact statements' in court; that the empathetic feelings they provoke tends to bias juries against the offender (Bandes 1996). Justice, which I shall assume is part of morality, should be 'blind'; that is, impartial. It is not just, and hence not moral, that one person should get a different punishment than another for the same offence simply because, at one of the trials, the jury was manipulated either by the expression of emotion by the perpetrator, or a more effective impact statement from the victim.

Third, 'empathy may be subject to unfortunate biases including cuteness effects' (Prinz 2011: 226). Young mammals, including children, are more likely to prompt our empathy than older mammals or other sorts of animal. Once again, egregious examples of this spring readily to mind. Aid charities tend to use pictures of children, and animal charities of puppies, to enlist our support. It is easier to motivate public opinion against the clubbing of seals than against the clubbing of rats. Once again, empirical support can be found. Gary Sherman and Jonathan Haidt, after reviewing the evidence, conclude that 'there is ample support for the claim that cuteness is an affective stimulus and that its effects on human cognition and behavior – however achieved – have important implications for morality' (Sherman and Haidt 2011: 6). Once again, these implications are worrying. If our morality is based on empathy, and empathy is systematically biased in favour of the cute, then our morality will be systematically biased in favour of the cute. However fond one is of the cute, such a bias would be contrary to justice and fairness.

Fourth, empathy 'may lead to preferential treatment' (Prinz 2011: 226). This is a broad category with many subcategories. Prinz himself mentions that 'empathy can be highly selective'; that 'empathy is particularly prone to in-group biases'; that 'empathy is prone to proximity effects'; and that 'empathy is subject to salience affects' (Prinz 2011: 226–7). One version of this has become known as the 'identifiable victim effect', here described by Paul Bloom:

The key to engaging empathy is what has been called 'the identifiable victim effect.' As the economist Thomas Schelling, writing forty-five years ago, mordantly observed, 'Let a six-year-old girl with brown hair need thousands of dollars for an operation that will prolong her life until Christmas, and the post office will be swamped with nickels and dimes to save her. But let it be reported that without a sales tax the hospital facilities of Massachusetts will deteriorate and cause a barely perceptible increase in preventable deaths – not many will drop a tear or reach for their checkbooks. (Bloom 2013)[6]

Empathy for a particular individual can mean we lose a sense of other deserving individuals, or even the background that led to the suffering of that particular individual. We empathize more with those with whom we have some personal relationship, or who are, for one reason or another, associated with us. This barely needs further discussion, but this has been demonstrated empirically on many occasions by Batson. In situations in which it would be just for each person to have an equal opportunity for some gain (such as medical treatment) people were willing to argue that certain individuals, with whom they had only a tenuous relationship, should get preferential treatment (Batson 2014: 47–52). If one generalizes from these experimental situations, as it would be legitimate to do, one can see that a morality based on empathy will favour personal attachments over justice and fairness.

Although, as we have seen, Batson takes empathy to provoke altruistic behaviour, he does not equate altruistic behaviour with moral behaviour. Indeed, in his writing on this, he takes a similar line to Prinz:

Altruism and moral motivation are distinct motives, each with its own ultimate goal: for altruism, the ultimate goal is to increase another's welfare; for moral motivation, to promote some moral standard, principle, or ideal (e.g., be fair, do no harm, produce the greatest good for the greatest number, do unto others...)...as a motive, empathy-induced altruism is neither moral nor immoral; it is amoral. Sometime it will encourage people to act in accord with their moral principles; at other times, to violate them. (Batson 2014: 46–7)

What Prinz and Batson are appealing to here is a contrast between morality ('which has the goal of promoting some universal and impartial moral standard, principle, or ideal' (Batson 2014: 53)) and empathy (which, as we have seen, is far from impartial).

The case for quarantining our moral thinking from the biases of empathy appears a strong one. Nonetheless, we should not let the sceptics have the last word. I shall put aside the first of my four headings; that empathy is not very motivating. Even were we to accept that typical empathic emotions might not have the power to move us in the way that, say, anger might, typical empathic emotions might nonetheless provide considerable motivating force. The second and third headings both claim that empathy can result in inappropriate motivations; either inappropriately caused (in the case of manipulation) or inappropriately directed (in the case of cuteness effects). In defence of the link between empathy and morality, we can perhaps borrow from Hume. It is not that we need to correct these motivations with a dose of independent moral thought; rather that we need to stand back from our motivations and consider them against a more neutral background (a 'common point of view'). We would need to achieve a sufficient distance from our motivating feelings so as to be able to correct their inappropriateness, while yet not being so distant such that they lose their hold on us. Whether we can achieve this ideal distance is not something I can sort out here. However, the door is not yet closed on a connection between empathy and moral behaviour.

It is the fourth heading, however, that is most philosophically interesting. Batson is certainly not alone in claiming that morality 'has the goal of promoting some universal and impartial moral standard, principle, or ideal'. Peter Singer regards the claim that morality is underpinned by 'a principle of impartiality, universalizability, equality, or whatever' as 'uncontroversial'. He takes this to entail that any partiality (of the sort brought about by empathy) is morally irrelevant (Singer 1972: 232). If a child has fallen into a pond next to me, and I am able to rescue him or her at little cost to myself, I am obliged to save that child. As considerations of proximity are morally irrelevant, for as long as there are children in the world threatened with death, we are equally obliged to donate that 'little cost' to a charity that can save a life (Singer 1997). Singer's ideas have had something of a revival recently, taken up by the movement for 'effective altruism', which holds that we are obliged to maximize the amount of good we can do in the world. One of the leaders of this movement, William MacAskill, has provided a vivid example of the conflict between empathic motivations and the demands of an impartial morality.

MacAskill is considering where he ought to donate a certain sum of money. He considers a donation to the Hamlin Fistula Hospital in Addis Ababa, Ethiopia. This is run by the Fistula Foundation, a charity dedicated to treating a truly awful medical condition which ruins the lives of some unfortunate women. He is motivated to do so as he has personal experience of this hospital:

> When I'd been in Ethiopia several years before, I'd visited this hospital. I'd hugged the women who suffered from this condition, and they'd thanked me for visiting them. It had been an important experience for me: a vivid first-hand demonstration of the severity of problems in the world. This was a cause I had a personal connection with.

However, this motivation conflicts with his impartialist view of morality:

> If I were to give to the Fistula Foundation rather than to charities I thought were more effective, I would be privileging the needs of some people over others for emotional rather than moral reasons. That would be unfair to those I could have helped more. If I'd visited some other shelter in Ethiopia, or any other country, I would have had a different set of personal connections. It was arbitrary that I'd seen this particular problem at close quarters. (MacAskill 2015: ch. 2)

This view of morality, as Singer acknowledged early on, is to some extent counter-intuitive. Indeed, MacAskill would argue that we should not favour charities such as our local hospice or Boy Scout troop as, clearly, less good would be done in the world by donating money to them than could be done by donating money to, for example, charities that distribute mosquito nets.

If moral theory takes this universal and impartial form we are all always under an obligation to maximize the amount we are able to give away, and then to give it away. This admirable consistency some find hard to accept. Some philosophers, of whom Bernard Williams is the most prominent example, have argued that this is so much the worse for this kind (or, indeed, in Williams's case, any kind) of moral theory: it is simply too far from our actual moral motivations for there to be any psychologically plausible way to bridge the gap (Williams 1985: 116–18). Given that any reader of this book is likely to earn, or have the potential to earn, more than the average income of his or her fellow human beings this would mean giving away, or planning to give away, a great deal of income. In addition, money should not be spent on non-moral pursuits, such as developing a taste in art, a taste in wine, pursuing an interest for its own sake or a career for the sake of interest in that career. There are some, including Singer and MacAskill, who accept this consequence and live their lives in this way, and who thus challenge the view that there is not 'any psychologically plausible' way to bridge the gap between theory and practice. Others have argued that to hold that we are under a constant obligation to promote some moral standard or ideal is to alienate ourselves from our own convictions and from the actions that flow from these convictions; convictions and actions that we may take to be what our lives are about (Williams 1973a: 49). Far from revealing that we are falling short in putting our own projects above that of pursuing an ideal, all that is revealed is, in the words of Richard Wollheim, that 'dreamland is crowded with moral philosophers' (Wollheim 1979: 21).

What I have outlined is two views of morality. The first takes moral motivation to have, in the words of Batson, 'the goal of promoting some universal and impartial moral standard, principle, or ideal'. The second rejects the standpoint that we are answerable to some universal and impartial ideal. The first, as we have seen, rejects empathy as a foundation for morality. The second, however, might find a place for it. It might be part of the convictions with which I identify that I improve the lot of my neighbours or help those in trouble who I have encountered in the course of my travels. The cause of my having these convictions might be that I have felt along with them; I feel a psychological bond with them, which I do not with others. Those who argue that we should be doing 'the most good we can do' would argue, of course, that having these feelings does not justify our acting on them. The counter-argument would be that such feelings give meaning to life, and cannot be trumped by moral theory. We use this fact, this fellow-feeling, to justify our acting partially rather than impartially.

Where does this leave us? At least this much can be said for empathy: taking the perspective of another, getting a sense of what it is like to be in their situation with their character, gives us a perspective on the world that is not our own. Coming to see the world as another sees it can put our own issues in perspective, lead to an appreciation of the problems of others and perhaps lead us to act for the sake of other people, not merely ourselves. In this chapter, I have argued that this leaves us some way from morality in two respects. First, the people empathy might lead us to take into consideration in our actions might not be those we ought to take into consideration in our actions. That is, our feelings of empathy might have been manipulated, or governed by morally irrelevant personal relations, or prompted by factors such as cuteness or physical attraction. Second, the larger questions of what constitutes a just resolution to a problem, or which power relationships are acceptable and which are unacceptable, are not questions for which empathy has answers. Indeed, we might sometimes need to overcome our feelings of empathy in order to address such questions in a morally adequate manner. I raised, but did not settle, the broader question as to the extent to which morality should or should not be impartial.

8

Empathy and Aesthetics

As we saw in chapter 1, the term 'empathy' had its origins in nineteenth-century German aesthetics. We left the story there at around the turn of the century. However, the aesthetic history of empathy did not stop at that time. I will look briefly at the aesthetic use of the term in Anglo-American philosophy in the early twentieth century.[1] This divides into two strands. The first was fundamentally experimental rather than theoretical, and concerned with the projection of movement rather than the projection of feeling. The second was principally pursued in Oxford, and was fundamentally theoretical, concerned with 'solving' the problem of beauty.

The first was pursued by the English writer Violet Paget who wrote under the name 'Vernon Lee'. Paget, or Lee, was an intriguing figure who wrote short stories, principally tales of the supernatural, and who was friends with, amongst others, Walter Pater and Henry James. In 1897, Lee and her collaborator, Clementine Anstruther-Thomson, published 'Beauty and Ugliness', an essay largely devoted to the physiological reactions of Anstruther-Thomson in front of works of art. At this time Lee had not read Lipps's work, and she was largely influenced by what she calls the 'Lange-James' account of the emotions, which identified emotions with bodily movements. The view put forward in 'Beauty and Ugliness' was that aesthetic appreciation is bound up with introspected perceptions of inner activity, some aspects of these changes subsequently being attributed to the object. (The genesis and nature of Lee's theory have been brilliantly explored by Carolyn Burdett 2011.) In 1912, Lee republished the essay, together with a number of other essays (Lee and Anstruther-Thomson 1912). By this time she had read Lipps and, despite an unflattering review he had published of the earlier essay, had moved away from a focus on introspecting activity to a more complicated view which married some of her earlier views with material she took from Lipps. Having said that, her book does contain some telling criticisms of Lipps. She rightly criticizes him for theory-building in isolation from the results of empirical psychology, and for the obscurity of his idea that the whole ego is projected into the object as opposed to attributions of states of the ego (Lee and Anstruther-Thomson 1912: 66, 103).

It is not clear how seriously Lee was taken by the academic establishment. She describes herself as 'a novice in psychology' (Lee and Anstruther-Thomson 1912: 64) and is disarmingly modest about her work:

> My aesthetics will always be those of the gallery and the studio, not of the laboratory. They will never achieve scientific certainty. They will be based on observation rather than experiment; and they will remain, for that reason, conjectural and suggestive. (Lee and Anstruther-Thomson 1912: viii)

Either for these reasons, or because it was difficult for a woman to be taken seriously in the academic environment, or for her pacifist stand in the First World War, Lee's influence declined. Having said that, there has recently been a revival of interest in her work. In addition to the paper by Burdett mentioned above, Susan Lanzoni has argued for the importance of her contribution to the development of the concept of empathy in turn-of-the-century psychology (Lanzoni 2009: 351).

The key figure in the reception of Lipps's work in Oxford was E. F. Carritt, a philosopher at University College who was unusual in having an interest in aesthetics. Carritt published a collection of writing in the history of aesthetics, which included what is, to date, the most extensive translations of Lipps into English (Carritt 1931). This includes a passage from Lipps where he seems to have articulated a problem which, even if not particularly precise, is central to discussions of beauty. He puts the problem thus: 'The sensible appearance of the beautiful object is the object of aesthetic satisfaction; but, just as surely, it is not the ground of that satisfaction' (Lipps 1903: 252). This can be understood against a background of finding a middle way between two unsatisfactory accounts of beauty: that which takes it to be an objective property of objects, and that which takes the judgement of taste ('that object is beautiful') to be an expression of a subjective state.

The first such account is that beauty is a property of an object much like any other property it might have. Hence, the beauty of a rose would have the same status as its colour (pink) or its being of the variety 'Omar Khayyam'. We can see what is unsatisfactory about this account by noticing two corollaries of it. The first is that, in principle, such facts can be proved: I could compare the rose to a colour swatch to prove that it was pink, or I could consult a shop receipt (or, more drastically, a definitive guide to varieties of rose) to prove that it was an Omar Khayyam. The second corollary is that we can learn such facts at second hand. If you tell me you have bought a pink rose or an Omar Khayyam rose, then (provided I trust you) it is reasonable for me to form my beliefs on the basis of your testimony. Both of these corollaries are problematic for the same reason: the account underplays the role of experience. As Kant said, offering me a proof would not put me in touch with beauty – 'there can be no rule by which someone could be compelled to acknowledge that something is beautiful' (Kant 1987: 215–16). If I cannot see the beauty, showing me a receipt where it is described as 'beautiful' will not help. The same is true of testimony; simply telling me that something is beautiful will not put me in a position to see its beauty.

The inadequacy of the first account might drive us in the direction of the second: that judgements of beauty are really disguised expressions of some subjective state, usually taken to be pleasure. On this second account, I look at the rose, it pleases me and I express my pleasure with the words 'that rose is beautiful'. The problem with this (as with all expressive accounts whether in aesthetics or ethics) is explaining the form of words I use. According to the account, I am simply expressing my pleasure. The form of words I use, however, seems to indicate a claim about the rose: it is *the rose* that is beautiful. Indeed, the form of words is a more accurate reflection of the situation than our speculative account. In making judgements of beauty, we are not simply expressing our own mental states. To quote from Kant again, 'It would be ridiculous if someone who prided himself on his taste tried to justify it saying: This object...is beautiful *for me*' (Kant 1987: 212). This account overplays the role of experience, and neglects the fact that we are making claims about an object: namely, that it (that very thing) is beautiful.

Lipps's solution is characteristically obscure:

> Aesthetic satisfaction consists in this; that it is satisfaction in an object, which yet, just so far as it is aesthetically enjoyed, is not myself but something objective. This is what is meant by Empathy: that the distinction between the self and the object disappears or rather does not yet exist. (Lipps 1903: 253)

Intriguingly, a fairly strong echo of these words is found in a passage from R. G. Collingwood (the same Collingwood we encountered in chapter 5), who was a pupil of Carritt. Collingwood's great work on aesthetics is his 1938 book, *The Principles of Art* (Collingwood 1945). Less well known is an earlier book (1925), *Outlines of a Philosophy of Art*. In this, Collingwood appears to adopt Lipps's view:

> The question has sometimes been raised, whether beauty is 'objective' or 'subjective', by which is meant, whether it belongs to the object and is by it imposed on the mind by brute force, or whether it belongs to the mind and is by it imposed on the object irrespective of the object's own nature...real beauty is neither 'objective' nor 'subjective' in any sense that excludes the other. It is an experience in which the mind finds itself in the object, the mind rising to the level of the object and the object being, as it were preadapted to evoke the fullest expression of the mind's powers. The experience of beauty is an experience of utter union with the object; every barrier is broken down, and the beholder feels that his own soul is living in the object, and that the object is unfolding its life in his own heart. (Collingwood 1925: 43)

Somehow the object brought about feelings in the observer, and the observer then wholly identified with the object. As this general approach was common currency at the time, it might be fanciful – despite the similarity of the language used – to suggest a direct link between Lipps and Collingwood. However, the link is made in Carritt's anthology where a footnote to the passage from Lipps directs us to the passage from Collingwood. As Collingwood is thanked by Carritt in the anthology's acknowledgements, we can assume that this was done with his approval.

Even granted that Collingwood was following Lipps, this seems to be the only significant statement of agreement with Lipps's view in Anglo-American aesthetics. Even as early as 1908, the view was being condemned for its obscurity (Anonymous 1908). Carritt himself considers and rejects the view for the same reason in 1914: 'We have here nothing but an attempt to explain in figurative language an unconscious process by which some beautiful objects may have become so' (Carritt 1949: 278–9). The aesthetic doctrine of empathy, in which observers gave objects life by a process of total identification of the ego, was replaced by less obscure, and psychologically more plausible, doctrines.[2]

The revival of interest in empathy in the past fifteen years has not featured much in aesthetics and the philosophy of art. There is, however, some interest and I shall consider two debates: the first broadly within the visual arts and the second in understanding fictions (some points from the first discussion carry over to the second). The first breaks down into a number of different issues, not always related. The second claims that in order to understand narratives, in particular, fictions, we need to empathize with the characters depicted therein.

This book so far has explored the various ways in which we can take on the perspective of another so as to understand them, or to exhibit transparent fellow-feeling with that other (as before, I shall refer to the other as 'the target'). We can do this in the context of perceiving the target in whatever situation they are in, or learning about the target and their situation and imagining that situation from their perspective. As there is no restriction on how I learn about the target's situation, there seems an easy generalization to figurative art.

To consider narrow empathy for the moment, faced with a distressed person, I might be prompted to feel empathy for him or her. There seems no reason, then, why being faced with a representation of a distressed person might not have the same effect. Dominic McIver Lopes makes the point in a paper to which we will shortly return:

> Pictures evoke experiences as of the scenes they represent. Call these experiences 'seeing-in'. To see a man in a photograph is to have an experience, sustained by the photograph, as of a man.... All figurative pictures sustain seeing-in in this sense. The claim is that the features of seeing that are responsible for evoking empathy are features with which seeing-in resembles face-to-face seeing. Empathic response picks up on the very same features, whether they figure in seeing-in or face-to-face seeing. (Lopes 2011: 119)

It is not only narrow empathy that carries across to figurative art. In chapters 3 and 4 we discussed 'low-level empathy' or 'motor mimicry'. When I witness you performing some action there is a sense in which my body mimics the performance of that action. It was central to the nineteenth-century debates that this is also true of visual representations of actions. It would be unsurprising, then, if these mechanisms were not operating when we looked at representational art. When we look at Rubens's *Descent from the Cross*, for example, we are made aware of the strain on those lifting Christ's heavy body down. Gregory Currie has attempted to add some detail to this thought and hence enrich our account of what it is to engage with the visual arts (Currie 2011). Currie considers empathic responses in the context of the worry that, as they are happenings that take place in the viewer, attending to them would, at best, be a distraction from attending to the work. He considers two responses to this. The first is to consider empathy as a mode of perception: 'the mechanisms which simulate state or process S, and which are activated by another person's being in S, or being depicted as being in S, constitute states of perceiving the other's being in S' (Currie 2011: 89). Currie rejects this: our usual senses are reliable at perceiving states of other people; our empathic responses are too irregularly correlated with the states of others, and, even if they are thus correlated, rely on the other senses as part of the perception. Rejecting our empathic responses as themselves perceptual is compatible, however, with those responses feeding into perception. Currie cites empirical studies which suggest that this connection between two mental systems in fact obtains: 'how things look is partly a function of inner motor processes, which must in that case have some causal connection to the visual system' (Currie 2011: 91).

This is an interesting distinction to which I will return when considering the role of empathy in our engaging with literature. That is, there are sub-personal systems (our 'inner motor processes') that, although they are not themselves part of our conscious awareness, are causal influences on our conscious awareness. One reason this is of interest is that those who work in art and aesthetics are generally interested in what to say at the conscious level: the level of the person, the person's mind and the person's understanding. There is a danger of theorists talking past each other; if those who insist on there being a role for empathy mean it at the sub-personal level, that might be compatible with those who deny there is such a role at the personal level. Here I simply raise the issue; I will return to it below.

This is not the only role for empathic mental states that Currie considers. A second borrows from the claim by Kendall Walton that we can use our own mental states to refer to the states of others. Currie illustrates this once more with his example of Rubens's painting:

> Part of an aesthetically aware response to *Descent from the Cross* is a vivid sense of bodily strain experienced by the mourners as they lower the dead Christ. And my capacity to think, of one of the figures, 'He feels thusly', where 'thusly' picks out a feeling of bodily contortion and strain which I am currently simulating, gives my thought about the figures a specificity and a vividness that they would not have if I had to rely on using a descriptive concept such as 'feels some unspecified tension in his arms and shoulders'. (Currie 2011: 93)

Our 'actual world' empathetic skills, motor mimicry, and other aspects of both broad and narrow empathy enrich our appreciation of at least figurative art. Furthermore, by exercising such skills, works of art can enrich our appreciation of the actual world. Once more, here is a quotation from Lopes:

> By representing situations and bringing in emotions in these ways, pictures contribute to empathic skill. Exercising a skill generally improves the skill. Pictures evoke episodes of empathy that are relevantly similar to extra-pictorial episodes of empathy: they exercise the same skill that gets exercised in extra-pictorial episodes of empathy. So they contribute to empathic skill. (Lopes 2011: 126)

This accounts for what our experiencing empathy when engaged with the visual arts has in common with our experiencing empathy when engaged with the world, and also how the former can aid the latter (what Lopes calls 'carry-over problem'). However, we might want to be more ambitious: to explain how experiencing the visual arts can make a *distinctive* contribution to our empathetic skill (this Lopes calls 'the difference problem'). That is, is there a way (or are there ways) in which our experience of empathy when engaged with the visual arts differs from that when we engage with the world, where the former might aid the latter?

To solve this problem, we would need to find something distinctive about the visual arts, that is, something that is true of the visual arts that is not true of the world generally, and show how this makes a contribution to our empathetic skills. One well-attested difference between our engagement with art and our engagement with the world is that in the latter we are limited by our environment, and our encounters take quotidian forms that are frequently unsatisfying. Art has neither of these limitations. Murray Smith makes this point in the course of a wide-ranging paper about how we use the arts to extend our emotional lives into the world:

> In what ways might empathy, then, be stretched and refined through its engagement with the narrative arts? In *scope* and *intensity*. Our ability to empathize is extended across a wide range of types of person, and sustained and intensified by virtue of the artificial, 'designed' environment of fictional experience. We are all limited, to a greater or lesser extent, in the opportunities we have to engage with situations, persons, and cultures different to a greater or lesser extent from our

own. For those who want to take it up, fiction – and once again, public narration more generally – affords a limitless horizon of opportunities for such engagement; the possibility of understanding 'from the inside' – that is, empathically imagining – human agents in social situations more or less radically different from our own emerges. (Smith 2011: 111)

Lopes draws on a more radical way in which the visual arts differ from the actual world to solve 'the difference problem'. It is true of works of art, in a way that it is not true of bits of the inanimate world, that scenes express emotions. Lopes's example is Géricault's *Raft of the Medusa*, in which the sea expresses 'malignant indifference' and the tiny ship almost out of sight on the horizon expresses 'blind indifference' (Lopes 2011: 130). Lopes claims that the expressive qualities of the scene can guide us to the emotion that the figures in the picture are expressing. In the case of the *Raft of the Medusa*, the sailors express despair and we are guided to see this as despair is the appropriate reaction to malignant indifference and blind indifference. Lopes's problem is that he can solve the carry-over problem (the empathetic skills we use in engaging with narrative art are those we use in engaging with the world) and he can solve the difference problem (the resources employed by works of art differ from those employed by the world), but not both together.

His solution to this is ingenious. First, he points to an analogy between that which he claims is distinctive of art – that scenes express emotions – and one way in which our emotions function in the world: namely, 'social referencing'. Social referencing occurs when a person uses someone else's emotional reaction to a situation as a clue to what their own response should be:

In social referencing one person uses another person's affective response to a situation in order to assess the situation, guide his behavior, and perhaps determine his own affective response. Children develop a capacity for this within their first year and it is fully in place by eighteen months. When put in an unfamiliar and ambiguous situation, they will try to keep within sight of their mother's face, they will engage in visual 'check back' behaviors, and they will inhibit play when she is preoccupied. When they do detect a significant expression on their mother's face, their behavior is profoundly modified. (Lopes 2011: 131)

Lopes's claim is that we use scene expression in a way analogous to that in which we use social referencing:

> We respond empathetically with some figures we see in pictures. Sometimes this response involves us seeing a scene as expressive, though the expression is not attributable to the figure. Since we do not normally see bits of the inanimate world as expressing anything, this is a distinctively pictorial response. Moreover, scene expression can play a referencing role, marking features of situations as warranting responses. The cognitive pay-off is that we learn to recognize situations as warranting certain responses, even when the expressive element is removed. (Lopes 2011: 133)

In this way, he is able to solve the 'carry-over' problem and the 'difference problem' together.

So far, the link between empathy and the visual arts has involved our using our empathetic skills to respond to the narrative content of pictures. This overlaps with the nineteenth-century discussion; as we know from chapter 1, Lipps did talk about responding to the form of the human figure. However, the core of the nineteenth-century discussion, carried over into Vernon Lee's work, lay in the *projection* of our mental states into works of art. As we saw in chapter 1, Robert Vischer borrowed the notion of projection from Karl Albert Scherner's book *Das Leben des Traums* (*The Life of the Dream*). That book influenced Freud, and Freud, in turn, was a huge influence on one of the significant philosophers of art of the twentieth century, Richard Wollheim. In Wollheim, we return to the idea that our engaging with a work of art is, at least in part, a matter of our projecting our mental states on to it.

Wollheim thinks there are 'three fundamental perceptual capacities that the artist relies upon the spectator to have and to use.' These are 'seeing in' (which delivers representational properties); 'expressive perception' (which delivers 'the power to express mental and internal phenomena'); and 'visual delight' ('the power to induce a special form of pleasure') (Wollheim 1987: 45). It is the second of these that will concern me here. Wollheim discussed expressive properties in a number of places, most definitively in his essay 'Correspondence, Projective Properties, and Expression in the Arts' (Wollheim 1991). At the centre of this account is our projecting our mental states on to objects.

In order to understand his views on expression, one first needs a grasp of what Wollheim means by 'projection'. He distinguishes two sorts of projection: simple projection and complex projection. The first is familiar from the psychoanalytic literature: a person cannot tolerate their melancholy (for example) so they project it on to some other person (or minded thing) in their environment. This has two consequences. Their feeling of melancholy is lessened, and they come to believe the person on whom they have projected their inner state is melancholic. Complex projection occurs when an inner state is projected on to the environment. Once again, the melancholy is lessened. However, the person does not come to believe the environment possesses some psychological property – that would be madness – but comes 'to look upon, or respond to, some part of the environment as melancholy' (Wollheim 1991: 151).

What appears to happen is as follows. A piece of art or nature has a certain kind of appearance that makes it particularly suitable as the recipient of the projection of our mental state.[3] We project our mental state and, once this is done, the piece of art or nature takes on a certain visual appearance to us: we do not believe that it literally possesses this mental state; rather, we see it as being 'of a piece' with our emotions. However, this cannot be the standard account of expressive properties in objects, as it would require that someone could only see objects as (for example) melancholy after a particular episode of projection. That simply seems far-fetched – we do not need to have been in a heightened emotional state to experience objects as expressive. Hence, Wollheim claims that we recognize a piece of nature as one 'on which we might have, or could have, projected this or that kind of feeling' (Wollheim 1991: 153–4). The experience of a piece of art or nature as expressive intimates its own history: that is, it intimates its origins in the kind of experience it is – an experience of the projection of an inner state on to art or nature. This, in itself, is sufficient to bring about the change in appearance, and imbue the object with projective properties.

What Wollheim's view has in common with discussions of empathy is the projection of our inner lives on to objects. 'Projecting on to' is different from 'projecting into'; there is no Lippsian notion of an identification of ourselves with the object. In this sense, the view is closer to that argued for by Currie; that our affective mechanisms underpin changes in our perceptions. Currie's account, however, does not involve projection and it is this element that (as with the earlier theorists) remains obscure. To begin with, the notion of 'complex projection' is Wollheim's invention, and is not found in the psychoanalytic literature (a point I owe to Malcolm Budd). That would not be a problem were the notion independently defensible, but it is problematic for several reasons. First, unlike the case of simple projection, there is no underlying reason for there to be a mechanism for the systematic projection of our emotions, whatever they might be, positive or negative, on to objects in our immediate environment. Second, Wollheim's concession that the spectator does not need to be experiencing the emotion makes it difficult to see that what is involved is a state of projection at all – what would there be to project (Budd 2001)?

Thus, we can see that the notion of empathy has reappeared in our theorizing about the visual arts in rather a haphazard and disjointed manner. Its use in the second area that I will be looking at, the philosophy of literature, is more systematic. As we have seen, empathizing with someone can take the form of simulating mental states, or generating affective states, by imagining being in their shoes. By common consent, engaging with fictional narratives is a matter of being prescribed to imagine their content.[4] This places us in the right ball-park; as we are imagining anyway, all that needs to be the case is that engaging with a fictional narrative involves not only imagining the content, but taking the perspective of one or more of the characters, so as to access their (fictional) mental lives.

It will be admitted on all sides that affective reactions play some role in our engaging with narratives. At a basic level, we can like some characters more than others; we can fear for people in danger, and feel dread at people's degradation. We move close to the claim that we engage empathetically if we hold that we imagine certain things are going on in the heads of characters; we try to work out what a fictional character is thinking or feeling.

There is a putative problem here (the problem is raised – albeit to make a different point – in McFee (2011: 206)). I shall illustrate this with an example from a fiction film, rather than a piece of written fiction, although the point generalizes. In an infamous scene from the film *The Shining*, we are faced with Wendy Torrance (the character played by Shelley Duvall) in obvious fear and distress. Narrow empathy requires that I feel the same emotion, or an appropriately related emotion, to that felt by the target. Wendy Torrance, being fictional, has no emotion. Hence, even if there are 'the very same features, whether they figure in seeing-in or face-to-face seeing', empathy cannot be possible; there is no emotion for our emotion to match. This has persuaded some that directly empathizing is not possible and something more indirect is needed.[5]

> When empathizing with fictional characters...there is no other existing being whose psychological processes one simulates. Instead, appreciation requires recognizing what psychological processes you are simulating – identifying your own affective or emotional condition – and also determining whether that condition is attributable to a fictional character with whom you are allegedly empathizing. (Feagin 1996: 101)

To illustrate what she means by this, Susan Feagin gives the following example. She considers the sentence from Virginia Woolf's *To the Lighthouse*: 'Mr. Ramsay, stumbling along a passage one dark morning, stretched his arms out, but Mrs. Ramsay having died rather suddenly the night before, his arms, though stretched out, remained empty.'[6] Feagin claims that she read this sentence 'with surprise and incredulity' and – and she gives good reasons for this claim – that these responses are 'in a sense, attributable to [Mr. Ramsay]' (Feagin 1996: 96–7). Hence, we have an instance in which we attribute one of our own mental states to a fictional character without doing what Feagin thinks impossible – that is, simulating the mental states of a fictional character. To put the point another way, the perspective of Mr Ramsay is never taken, but rather an emotion caused by the sentence induces, deliberately one supposes, an emotion plausibly attributed to the character. This might happen – indeed, I am sure it does happen – but the absence of perspective-taking disqualifies it in my eyes as an instance of empathy.

Is there really a problem with simulating the mind of a fictional character? To sort this out fully would require a full account of our psychological engagement with fictional characters (the standard account, for good reason, is Walton (1990)). However, I hope I can say enough to allay the problem by sorting out the scope of the 'in a fiction...' operator. I shall put the point in terms of literary fiction (although, once again, the claim generalizes across fictions in all media). It is true in a fiction that characters have emotional lives. In literary fiction, they often have very rich emotional lives – consider Elizabeth Bennett or Dorothea Brooke. Part of our engagement with fiction is engaging with these emotional lives. Creators of fiction, whether involving Wendy Torrance or the two heroines just mentioned, give the characters 'the very same features' as they would have in the non-fictional world, and expect us to use 'the very same skills' to move from these features to an engagement with their emotional lives. All this happens *within* the fiction; none of it requires that we postulate an absurdity such as an actual emotional life for a fictional character.

Even if it is possible for empathy to take place within our engagement with fiction, is there any evidence that empathy does take place? Zanna Clay and Marco Iacoboni argue that there is. They take as a datum to be explained that 'the feeling of connecting with...fictional characters can be an authentic and enduring experience'. Their explanandum is that 'the foundations of this sense of connection lie primarily in our profound capacity for empathy, where the reader comes to experience the thoughts, actions, and perceptions of the fictional characters as if they were experiencing themselves' (Clay and Iacoboni 2011: 313). They take this to be a form of low-level empathy; 'neural mirroring mechanisms may underlie the ability to connect emotionally with fictional others in the same way that they help us to relate to real people in our daily lives' (Clay and Iacoboni 2011: 314). This view could only be accepted, however, if we accept two rather tendentious claims: that mirror neurons are activated when we read representations, and that mirror neurons do actually underlie the ability to connect emotionally with others.

Let us grant that observing an action or emotion can cause, in the observer, a pattern of neural activity that resembles part of the neural activity of the actor or emoter. What Clay and Iacoboni need is something stronger than this; that reading about an action can cause, in the reader, a pattern of neural activity that would resemble part of the neural activity of the actor or emoter were there such an actor or emoter. In other words, their account requires that mirror neurons are activated by representations as much as they are by face-to-face encounters. They admit that 'there is no direct data in support of our claim' (Clay and Iacoboni 2011: 326), offering instead evidence that rather loosely links premotor cortex activity with the development and use of language. They conclude that:

> When we read about a fictional character experiencing a powerful emotion, neural mechanisms of mirroring may re-evoke the neural representation of the facial gestures and bodily postures typically associated with that emotion, and trigger activity in emotional brain centres such that we end up experiencing the emotion associated with those facial gestures and bodily postures. (Clay and Iacoboni 2011: 317)

I remain sceptical about the claim, but let us grant it for the sake of argument. We saw in chapter 4 that even if we grant the existence of mirror neurons, they are too far back in our processing to be sure that they form the basis of even low-level empathy. This worry applies with equal or greater force here (greater, as the neural patterning will, if anything, be weaker than the face-to-face case). However, even if we accept it, it is unclear what Clay and Iacoboni have shown. It is part of their case that the mirror neurons of the reader are activated only once they know what action the fictional character is performing or what emotion they are feeling. Hence, the mirror neurons are not playing an epistemic role; they are not enabling the reader to grasp anything they do not already know. Mirror neurons are not part of a reader's consciousness, so they do not figure in the reading experience. Even if all the hypotheses are accepted we only have the claim that a mirroring response, at a very primitive level, may be part of the causal process by which a reader comes to form conscious experiences. This may be too weak a claim even to qualify as low-level empathy.

An argument for empathy occurring at a less primitive level has been made by Amy Coplan. Coplan describes experiments that seem to show that readers 'tend to adopt a position within the spatiotemporal framework of narratives that is based on the position of the protagonist', and also that 'readers often process the emotional implications of narrative events from the standpoint of one of the protagonists' (Coplan 2004: 141, 142). The experiments take the form of asking readers to recall pieces of the text, or answer questions, and showing that they have readier access to information consonant with the relevant perspective than information that is not. This appears to show, as Coplan says, that 'readers' engagement with fictional narratives involves taking up the perspective of the characters' (Coplan 2004: 143). As with the hypothesis regarding mirror neurons, one might wonder what conclusions to draw from Coplan's work. Certainly, something seems to be going on in the reader's head such that the reader is taking the perspective of the character, but it is not clear that this features in anything we might call *understanding*. I shall return to this point below before examining one further argument for our employing empathy when reading texts: that of Greg Currie.

Currie is one of those who has argued for the view that engaging with fictions is a matter of imagining their content. More precisely, writers of fictional propositions intend that we imagine those propositions on the basis of a recognition of that intention (Currie 1990: 30). This he calls 'primary imagining'. However, such imagining seems a bit bare as an account of what it is that we get out of fiction. Hence, Currie supplements it with what he calls 'secondary imagining': 'Secondary imagining occurs when we imagine various things so as to imagine what is true in the story' (Currie 1995: 152). Currie goes on to provide an example:

> It is when we are able, in imagination, to feel as the character feels that fictions of character take hold of us. This process of empathetic re-enactment of the character's situation is what I call secondary imagining. As a result of putting myself, in

imagination, in the character's position, I come to have imaginary versions of the thoughts, feelings and attitudes I would have were I in that situation. Having identified those thoughts, feelings and attitudes ostensively, I am then able to imagine that the character felt *that* way. That is how secondary imagining is a guide to primary imagining. (Currie 1995: 153–4)

Currie's example is of 'a certain character walking down a dark street': 'If the dark street hides something threatening, the character who walks it may have thoughts, anxieties, visual and auditory experiences and bodily sensations that it would be important for readers to imagine something about' (Currie 1995: 153).

I have argued elsewhere that, if Currie is right that readers do indulge in secondary imagining, it will occur as much for non-fiction as it would for fiction (Matravers 2014: 30–1). There is no reason to think that readers get to grips with the content of non-fictional texts in a systematically different way from that in which they get to grips with the content of fictional texts. So let us generalize the claim to be that we perform 'empathetic re-enactment of the character's situation' whether that character is non-fictional or fictional. Is that claim true?

If we do perform such a re-enactment, it is not clear that, in the usual case, we do so consciously. Certainly, we are able to; we can consciously take on the perspective of one of the characters we are reading about. For example, one might be reading about George Macartney's diplomatic mission to China, his reception by the Emperor Qianlong and the issue of whether or not to kowtow. One can put oneself, in imagination, in Macartney's position, visualize the splendour of the Qing court, the strangeness of the customs and the mutual incomprehension of what is required in terms of etiquette. Such a phenomenologically rich activity will occur above the level of consciousness, and will possibly require that we pause in our reading – at least, it is not clear that we can perform two such mentally intensive activities simultaneously. It is more likely that Currie means that we perform secondary imagining unconsciously, or, at least, semi-consciously. That is, we may be dimly aware of the activity going on in a way that enriches the experience of reading.

It is not clear, however, that Currie is right to think secondary imagining goes on as we read. Noël Carroll has made the case against:

> We do not typically emote with respect to fictions by simulating a character's mental state; rather...we respond emotionally to fiction from the outside. Our point of view is that of an observer of a situation and not...that of a participant in the situation. When a character is about to be ambushed, we feel fear for her; we do not imagine ourselves to be her and then experience 'her' fear. (Carroll 2001: 311–12)[7]

There are typically two salient differences between encountering the world via a representation and encountering the world face-to-face. The first is that when we encounter the world via a representation, we are usually told what is going on; we do not need to work it out. The second is that, unless the text specifically instructs us to do so, representations tend not to encourage us to imagine the scene from the perspective of a particular character.[8] Consider the following passage from F. Scott Fitzgerald's *Tender is the Night*:

> In the spring of 1917, when Doctor Richard Diver first arrived in Zurich, he was twenty-six years old, a fine age for a man, indeed the very acme of bachelorhood. Even in war-time days, it was a fine age for Dick, who was already too valuable, too much of a capital investment to be shot off in a gun. Years later it seemed to him that even in this sanctuary he did not escape lightly, but about that he never fully made up his mind – in 1917 he laughed at the idea, saying apologetically that the war didn't touch him at all. Instructions from his local board were that he was to complete his studies in Zurich and take a degree as he had planned. (Fitzgerald 2005: 109)

There is no reason to think that we are required to empathize with Richard Diver, or indeed to do anything but – in Currie's terms – imagine the propositions expressed by the sentences on the page. My point is that this is not at all uncharacteristic of passages we encounter in narratives; we are simply given information that we absorb as part of the story.

Currie might admit that we do not indulge in secondary imagining in this case, but legitimately complain that this was not the kind of case that he meant. His example concerns a character engaging with the world, rather than a state of affairs being described. Let us then consider another example, this time from Alexandre Dumas's *The Three Musketeers*:

> Encouraged by this invitation, D'Artagnan followed the duke, who closed the door after him. The two found themselves in a small chapel covered with a tapestry of Persian silk worked with gold, and brilliantly lighted with a vast number of candles. Over a species of altar, and beneath a canopy of blue velvet, surmounted by white and red plumes, was a full-length portrait of Anne of Austria, so perfect in its resemblance, that D'Artagnan uttered a cry of surprise on beholding it. One might believe the queen was about to speak. On the altar, and beneath the portrait, was the casket containing the diamond studs. (Dumas 1974: 216)

Once again, it is difficult to see what information is unavailable to us without secondary imagining. Furthermore, if we do exercise our imaginations, over and above primary imagining, it is difficult to see why we should imagine from the point of view of any of the characters involved, rather than simply imagine the scene unfolding before us (in the terms introduced by Richard Wollheim, it is difficult to see why we should imagine centrally rather than acentrally (Wollheim 1986: 74)). Readers do not, surely, partake in D'Artagnan's surprise at the portrait as much as imagine that D'Artagnan is surprised at the portrait – or, at the extreme, imagine D'Artagnan's surprise at the portrait.

In all three of the theorists we have looked at – Clay and Iacoboni, Coplan, and Currie – the issue is raised concerning the relation between what goes on unconsciously (or even sub-personally) and the reader's awareness. It might be that the psychological processes described, if they occur, feed into conscious awareness. That is, they could be part of what causes the reader to sympathize with certain characters or react emotionally in certain ways. What we run up against here are two different approaches to the study of reading. One approach, a distinctively psychological approach, attempts to uncover the mechanisms that take us from a string of words on the page to a grasp of what those words mean. This is aptly described in a book that attempts to give an overview of the area:

> Most of the analysis and research...is based on the assumption that readers have the goal of identifying the apparent point or message of the narrator. Our justification for the focus on this one goal is that it is likely to be salient for most readers most of the time. (Bortolussi and Dixon 2003: 243)

Clearly, attempting to solve this problem will involve an investigation of mechanisms (whether unconscious or sub-personal) and the kinds of experiments described by Coplan. The second approach, the critical approach, will be interested in what can reasonably be called a reader's *understanding* of a text (see McFee 2011). There are a raft of issues here of which I will mention two.

First, as the psychological approach assumes a very minimal goal of the reader, there is no need to distinguish between different sorts of reader as all readers will share this minimal goal. However, beyond this minimal goal, reading literature is a skill. It would be absurd to think (and I am sure that nobody does think) that every reader's experience of some literary work will be the same. Skilled readers tend to read in a many-layered way, paying attention to the surface properties of the language, the unfolding story, the sympathies of the narrator, the different perspectives, needs and interests of the characters, and so on virtually without limit. Even were an unskilled reader and a skilled reader to perform identically on the various psychological tests, that would tell us little if anything about their experience and understanding of the text. Second, once the question of understanding is raised – is Prince Andrei a sympathetic figure, and to what extent does the character of Pierre unify Tolstoy's narrative? – the sub-personal mechanisms have been left far behind. One could, in attempting to think through, for example, Prince Andrei's apparently harsh treatment of his wife, deliberately take on first Prince Andrei's perspective and then the perspective of 'the little princess'. One could reflect on the significance of certain episodes, or look for evidence – in certain telling phrases – for the sympathies of the narrator. Literary understanding tends to be a self-conscious endeavour and the role of empathy in such an understanding stands at some remove from the kinds of role discussed by Clay, Iacoboni, Coplan and Currie.

Despite the historical roots of the modern concept of empathy being in aesthetics, I have not found much of a role for it in our appreciation of either visual art or narrative. This does not mean that we cannot stop to imagine what the world is like from the perspective of some depicted figure. It is only that empathy does not seem central to our appreciation of art or literature. This is because art and literature are more in the business of presenting us with a world to contemplate, rather than inviting us to construct a world for ourselves.

9
Afterword

As we have seen, the concept of empathy has had a strange history. It emerged out of nineteenth-century German philosophy, and had a brief flourishing in the Anglo-American world before the First World War. It appeared here and there (particularly in Collingwood) and was revived towards the end of the century as a position in the Philosophy of Mind. It was then taken up in various other domains, not always in the service of clarity.

What should we expect of the debates around empathy in the future? As we have seen, in contemporary philosophy empathy appears in both descriptive and normative guises. In the former, there are two pressing challenges. The first is the failure to agree on a meaning for the term, and even a failure to agree on the nature of the relevant mental phenomena. Such problems have led to attempts at greater precision by replacing 'empathy' with terms such as 'simulation'. However, such terms have themselves suffered similar problems, and have in turn been replaced by other terms. This is not to say that those responsible for attempting to do too much with the term are blameworthy. As Jane Heal has said about replacing the term 'simulation', 'it is no kind of criticism of proponents of simulation that they did not at the start of the debate anticipate all the possible complexities and distinctions which it would later prove useful to note' (Heal 1988:

112). We should not conclude from the fact that 'empathy' is prone to splinter under pressure that we have exhausted what the term can do for us. As we have seen, the heart of the matter, the imaginative occupation of the perspective of another, is a fundamental human capacity that underpins many of our epistemological practices. In particular, the rich tapestry of theorizing that has attempted to provide an alternative to the 'theory-theory' approach to interpersonal understanding has been especially valuable.

The second challenge ties the fate of empathy to a broader debate in the philosophy of mind. A view in philosophy, which I shall broadly refer to as 'the sociocultural view', does not dispute the importance of our capacity to occupy the perspective of another, but it does dispute the link between this capacity and our attribution of mental states to the other. Perhaps the best worked-out version of this view is that of Daniel Hutto. In his book, *Folk Psychological Narratives*, Hutto rejects the standard view of interpersonal understanding, a view common to both theory theory and simulation theory (Hutto 2008). I shall briefly review some of the key claims that are particularly relevant to our earlier discussions, although, as soon becomes evident, Hutto's claims only really make sense when considered as elements of the comprehensive view of which they are a part.

It is easy to slip into the thought that interpersonal understanding is a matter of making sense of people's actions by attributing propositional attitudes to them; particularly, beliefs and desires. To return to an earlier example, we might wonder why Jane has left her chair and is heading to the café. We satisfy ourselves if we work out that her action is caused by a belief that there is coffee to be had in the café and the desire for a cup of coffee. This form of explanation is what Hutto calls 'folk psychology': 'the practice of making sense of a person's actions using belief/desire propositional attitude psychology' (Hutto 2008: 3). His target is the claim that the primary business of folk psychology is 'third personal'. That is, he does not think the model I have been presupposing is correct. He does not think that interpersonal understanding is a matter of an observer attributing 'inner states' to a target, whether by the use of some implicit theory, or via a simulation of their mental mechanisms.

Even enthusiasts for folk-psychological explanations should agree that explaining people's actions is more than a matter of attributing belief/desire pairs. Not only can such pairs be understood as reasons for action only against a broader grasp of the agent's mental states, but the explanation of someone's actions might not refer to beliefs and desires at all. Rather, their actions could be explained by their being depressed, drunk, in the grip of some irrational state, driven by the wish that things could be otherwise, and so on and so forth. Nonetheless, the claim that we explain actions by attributing beliefs and desires, where those are thought of as mental states that cause and rationalize the actions, is common to most of the theorists I have considered in this book. Hutto has a barrage of arguments to counter this view. There are negative arguments that the view is unsustainable on its own terms, and positive arguments for his alternative. Here is one of the arguments that picks up on some of my earlier discussion. In chapter 3, I considered both our everyday explanations of people's actions which happen below the level of conscious awareness and our deliberate and conscious attempts to explain actions which puzzle us. Hutto argues that there is a more plausible alternative to folk psychology in the first case, and that folk psychology is not suited to the second. It is not suited to the second because such an explanation would be unreliable. If the person's actions are sufficiently outré to provoke conscious puzzlement, the causes of their actions may well be beyond the reach of a purely third-personal statement. Actions that provoke puzzlement are generally those that are irrational, that do not stem from the person's settled dispositions (they are 'out of character'), or stem from misinformation. These are just the sorts of characteristics, says Hutto, that make the roots of the action unreachable from the third-person standpoint.

The more plausible alternative to our everyday explanations does not make any attribution of beliefs and desires at all. Rather, we fit people's actions into familiar patterns; stories we tell that make sense of patterns of behaviour: 'Folk psychology just is the practice of making sense of intentional action by means of a special kind of narrative, those that are about or feature a person's reasons' (Hutto 2008: 7). The practice of giving reasons is not the practice of attributing content-bearing inner states. The practice is, rather, sociocultural; a matter of working with certain sorts of narrative – folk-psychological narratives. Hutto gives an example:

> Imagine that you see a man approaching the closed door of a shop while struggling with bags of groceries. We would hardly be surprised to see him put these down in order to open it or for him to wait until someone came to his aid. Should we suppose that our lack of surprise indicates that we were predicting, albeit tacitly, that this man might do either of these things? We might suppose that a tacit mentalistic prediction is unnecessary precisely because we already know what to expect from others and they know what to expect from us in such familiar social circumstances. To anticipate this set of actions I need to know or assume nothing about the particular mindset of this individual. (Hutto 2008: 6)

It is important to note that Hutto is not putting forward the weak thesis that there are more ways of getting to the inner states of individuals than theory theory or simulation. Rather, he is putting forward the strong thesis that giving reasons is not a matter of divining inner states at all. To understand why he takes this view, we need to understand how we develop our folk-psychological capacities. We work ourselves up to being folk psychologists in two stages. In the first stage, we are limited to the employment of what he calls 'unprincipled embodied engagements' (Hutto 2008: 101–28). We simply are sensitive to some of the ways the world is, including some of the ways that people are. Although this might well involve an intentional attunement to the world and to other people, such intentional attitudes are not themselves propositional attitudes; nor do they involve the attribution of propositional attitudes to others (Hutto 2008: 45). The second stage happens with the development of language. With the external prop of language, we are able to expand our thoughts considerably. In particular, we are able to use folk psychology (that is, understand the actions of others using a framework incorporating beliefs and desires) through participating in a particular narrative practice; that of engaging with stories about people who act for reasons. Once again, this can all be put in place without the need to attribute to others content-bearing inner states.

This is not the place to attempt a complete assessment of this attempt to displace empathy (at least, in its forms as simulation) from the position I have given it in interpersonal understanding. I shall, however, make two points. The first point is that there is some overlap between Hutto's view and the simulationist view. Hutto's first stage – the 'unprincipled embodied engagements' – is very similar to what Goldman calls 'low-level empathy' and Stueber calls 'basic empathy'. Hutto happily makes use of 'resonance systems' that encompass mirror neurons, emotional contagion, motor mimicry and goal emulation; processes that fall short of engaging in pretence or attributing mental states (Hutto 2008: 114–15). For Goldman and Stueber, such processes build to 'high-level' or 're-enactive' empathy, which involves the attribution of mental states. Hutto, of course, does not follow them in this. There is also some overlap at Hutto's second stage, where we become users of folk psychology through our engaging with narratives. Hutto's claim is that we make sense of others at the level of talk; by asking them for the story of why they did what they did. However, our grasp of what they tell us is a reason for their action depends upon viewing it against the background of other attitudes they have. This raises the frame problem, as there is no way, from the outside, that we can know which of those attitudes is relevant. Hutto's solution to this will be familiar: 'we are able to predict what another is likely to think about any given topic by co-cognizing with them' (Hutto 2008: 140). In short, Hutto is committed to some degree of simulation – that to which Heal's thesis of co-cognition commits him. However, as he rightly says and as Heal would agree, co-cognition will fall short of what is needed to make sense of the actions of others. Unlike the simulation theorists, Hutto thinks the shortfall is made up by engaging in narrative practices.

I said above that the fate of the model of empathy I have been using rests on a broader debate in the philosophy of mind. The crucial difference between Hutto and his opponents is the issue of whether postulating mental states, in the form of inner states that cause and rationalize behaviour, is or is not necessary for the satisfactory explanation of actions. Hutto and his fellow sociocultural theorists claim it is not; theory theorists and simulation theorists claim that it is. I cannot hope to sort this out here, or even to say anything that will take us closer to such a resolution. I will, however, venture the observation (and this is my second point) that, put in such a way, this looks to be a new form of an older debate. To the extent that it is, the sociocultural theorists might be vulnerable to the arguments from their opponents in that older debate (Davidson 1963). However this Homeric struggle is resolved, it is certainly true that the sociocultural theorists have stimulated a re-examination of some of the fundamental tenets of accounts of interpersonal understanding, including those that rely on empathetic mechanisms.

Away from the descriptive uses of 'empathy', the normative claims that are made on behalf of the concept – that we ought to be more empathetic – also seem in rude health. I began this book by quoting Barack Obama's call for an end to 'the empathy deficit'. In one way this ties into a contemporary desire for a less individualistic approach to the world, to move away from *homo economicus* (rational individuals in pursuit of their own self-interest) as the benchmark for rational behaviour. As many writers over many years have pointed out, human beings are not really like that (or, at least, most of us are not); human beings have desires to further the advance of other people for their own sake, and many of our actions are directed to that end. For those, such as President Obama, who would like to persuade people to be more altruistic, the call to empathize is a powerful one. It is the theme of Roman Krznaric's *Empathy: A Handbook for Revolution*, in which he argues that we should ditch the old model of rational behaviour in favour of becoming '*homo empathicus*' and inspire a world-wide revolution (Krznaric 2014: no pagination).

As we saw in chapter 7, matters are not that simple. Even if we grant that empathy leads to altruism, altruism is not morality. Indeed, the direction towards greater altruism might be the direction away from morality for two reasons. First, empathy is, by its very nature, partial; we empathize more with those who are closer to us than those who are further away. It is not moral to give a rationed university place to one with whom we empathize, rather than the one who is the most deserving. Second, the big questions of power and the distribution of resources are settled by the determinations of justice, and it is (at best) unclear whether empathy has a role to play in that realm. However, there are countervailing pressures. Even if altruism is not sufficient for morality, it may well be, if not necessary, at least a way out of a focus on our own concerns. To that extent, as psychologists such as Martin Hoffman have argued, the emphasis placed on empathy by the likes of President Obama is a sensible way to achieve greater mutual understanding. Even if greater mutual understanding will not necessarily lead to better moral behaviour, it is a plausible station on the way to that outcome.

Thus, we come to the end of our trip around contemporary debates on empathy. At times, my tone has been a slightly sceptical one. The promises made by empathy have sometimes not been redeemed, or, in redeeming them, the concept has changed its shape and become something else. However, provided those who work on empathy are clear what they mean by the term, there is still useful work that can be done. It is no surprise that so many are attracted to the notion; the thought that we can genuinely share another's perspective, occupy another's mind and escape the tyranny of self, is a very beguiling one.

Notes

Chapter 1 Introduction: Some Historical Preliminaries

1 There is a substantial literature on this. For a discussion, see Abramson (2001).
2 See Griswold (2006: Part 1).
3 The aesthetic history of the term is expertly traced in Guyer (2014: ch.10).
4 The underrated Hulme was blown to bits by a German shell in 1917.
5 Jahoda translates the title as 'Einfühlung, Inner Imitation, and Organic Feelings' (Jahoda 2005: 154).
6 My discussion here is drawn directly from an excellent paper by Gustav Jahoda (2005).
7 A fellow sceptic is Noël Carroll (2011: 163). For a list of the ways in which 'empathy' is currently understood, which is not claimed to be exhaustive, see Coplan (2011: 4).

Chapter 2 Some Conceptual Preliminaries

1 Most sides to the debate agree that 'simulation' is an unhelpful term, as it also means too many things to too

many people. However, as I am only giving an overview I shall continue with the term, marking relevant distinctions where necessary. Nichols and Stich give a helpful taxonomy (Nichols and Stich 2003: 133–4).

2 Heal's caveat, concerning 'misleading features', is well taken. The analogy is limited in various ways, particularly, as she is well aware, with respect to her own view. See Heal 1988: 111 and *passim*.

3 To multiply Smiths, Murray Smith makes the same distinction using the labels 'mind-reading' and 'mind-feeling' (Smith 2011: 114).

Chapter 3   Empathy as Simulation

1 For doubts about the extent to which the 'generate and test' method (or, as they call it, the 'analysis by synthesis' method) can generalize, see Nichols and Stich (2003: 139).

2 Goldie gives two further conditions, but we shall not go into those here.

3 An awareness that one has to be careful with money, no matter what one's disposition, will be more like the first than the second.

Chapter 4   A Priori and A Posteriori Empathy

1 Not all participants to the debate accept Heal's view. It is forcefully rejected in Nichols and Stich (1998), although those points are somewhat answered in Goldman (2006: 176–8). Heal still holds to the view (Heal 2013).

2 Heal has written a critical notice of the book, including reflections on the relation between Goldman's project and her own (Heal 2010).

3 See: <http://edge.org/3rd_culture/ramachandran/ramach andran_p1.html>.

4 Although Heal's suggestion was meant only as an alternative to the representation provided by Stich and Nichols rather than something she endorsed, recent work has

suggested her description is the more accurate (Matravers 2014). Indeed, there is something counter-intuitive in thinking that inference can only be performed on beliefs (or pretend beliefs); that is, that 'imagining that p' is synonymous with 'imagining believing that p'.

Chapter 5   Re-enacting the Thoughts of Others

1   Fortunately, there is one such of which I have made extensive use: Dray (1999).
2   Although I am following Stueber here, my reconstruction of the argument in Collingwood is different from his and he might well not agree with it.

Chapter 6   Empathy and the Emotions

1   That our imaginations can work independently of our wills is a feature of Kendall Walton's important work in this area. See Walton (1990).
2   S. T. Coleridge: 'Dejection: An Ode'.

Chapter 7   Empathy and Ethics

1   For an attempt to formulate an ethical theory based on empathy, that (in part, at least) embraces this partiality, see Slote (2007).
2   Just how complicated can be seen in Abramson (1999) (to whom I am grateful for help on this and related points).
3   Apart, that is, from the specialist field of the philosophy of evolutionary biology (Sober and Sloan Wilson 1999).
4   The lecture is available here: <https://www.youtube.com/watch?v=v79tL7uYTrA>.
5   The studies he cites are Underwood and Moore (1982) and Eisenberg, Fabes et al. (1989).
6   The reference is to Schelling (1968).

Chapter 8 Empathy and Aesthetics

1 The history is covered in Guyer (2014: ch.10).

2 Although, intriguingly, I came across the following exchange in a popular novel of 1946 by Michael Innes:

> 'In a manner of speaking,' said Mr Neff, 'you go right into a picture like that and move about in it.' He turned with sudden challenge to Meredith. 'Isn't that so?'
>
> 'Oh, undoubtedly.'
>
> 'It's as if you were exploring it with all your muscles ever so slightly moving, so that there's a sort of dance going on way inside yourself that's like all the movements in the picture. Isn't that so?' And again Mr Neff looked challengingly at his guest.
>
> Meredith was highly pleased. It was really remarkable, he thought, that this untutored person should so accurately describe what aestheticians call the theory of empathy. (Innes 1946: 278–9)

This is perhaps less intriguing when one learns that Michael Innes was J. I. M. Stewart, an Oxford don. Thanks to Vanessa Perry for lending me the book.

3 Wollheim oscillated between giving the same account for art and nature, and giving different accounts.

4 I do not share this view, but that difference does not matter for this discussion. What does matter is that the discussion is framed in terms of engaging with fictions, when, if it applies at all, it applies to all narratives (Matravers 2014).

5 Feagin may since have changed her mind; the view is not apparent in her excellent text (Feagin 2011).

6 Feagin gives the following reference: Virginia Woolf, *To the Lighthouse* (1927), p. 194.

7 Quoted in Coplan (2004: 147). I have used Coplan's condensation of Carroll's text.

8 These, and other points, are made in Kieran (2003).

Bibliography

Abramson, K. (1999). Correcting Our Sentiments About Hume's Moral Point of View. *The Southern Journal of Philosophy* XXXVII: 333–61.

Abramson, K. (2001). Sympathy and the Project of Hume's Second Enquiry. *Archiv fur Geschichte der Philosophie* 83(1): 45–80.

Anonymous (1908). Beauty and Expression. *The Edinburgh Review*: 458–86.

Bandes, S. (1996). Empathy, Narrative, and Victim Impact Statements. *The University of Chicago Law Review* 63(2): 361–412.

Barker, J. (ed.) (2006). *The Brontes: A Life in Letters*. London: Folio Society.

Batson, C. D. (2014). Empathy-Induced Altruism and Morality: No Necessary Connection. In H. L. Maibom (ed.), *Empathy and Morality*. Oxford: Oxford University Press, 41–58.

Batson, C. D., N. Ahmad and D. A. Lishner (2012). Empathy and Altruism. In S. J. Lopez and C. R. Snyder (eds), *The Oxford Handbook of Positive Psychology*. Oxford: Oxford University Press, 417–24.

Batson, C. D. and L. L. Shaw (1991). Evidence for Altruism: Towards a Plurality of Prosocial Motives. *Psychological Inquiry* 2(2): 107–22.

Battaly, H. D. (2011). Is Empathy a Virtue? In A. Coplan and P. Goldie (eds), *Empathy: Philosophical and Psychological Perspectives*. Oxford: Oxford University Press, 277–302.

Blackburn, S. (1995). Theory, Observation, and Drama. In M. Davies and T. Stone (eds), *Folk Psychology*. Oxford: Blackwell, 274–89.

Bloom, P. (2013) The Baby in the Well: The Case Against Empathy. *The New Yorker.* Available at: <http://www.newyorker.com/magazine/2013/05/20/the-baby-in-the-well>.

Bloom, P. (2014). Against Empathy. *The Boston Review*, September. Available at: <http://bostonreview.net/forum/paul-bloom-against-empathy>.

Borg, E. (2007). If Mirror Neurons are the Answer, What was the Question? *The Journal of Consciousness Studies* 14(8): 5–19.

Bortolussi, M. and P. Dixon (2003). *Psychonarratology.* Cambridge: Cambridge University Press.

Boucher, D. (1997). The Significance of R. G. Collingwood's Principles of History. *Journal of the History of Ideas* 58(2): 309–30.

Budd, M. (2001). Wollheim on Correspondence, Projective Properties and Expressive Perception. In R. van Gerwen (ed.), *Richard Wollheim on the Art of Painting.* Cambridge: Cambridge University Press, 101–11.

Burdett, C. (2011). The Subjective Inside Us Can Turn Into the Objective Outside: Vernon Lee's Psychological Aesthetics. *Interdisciplinary Studies in the Long Nineteenth Century* 12: 1–31.

Carritt, E. F., ed. (1931). *Philosophies of Beauty: From Socrates to Robert Bridges Being the Sources of Aesthetic Theory.* Oxford: Clarendon Press.

Carritt, E. F. (1949). *The Theory of Beauty.* London: Methuen.

Carroll, N. (2001). *Beyond Aesthetics: Philosophical Essays.* Cambridge: Cambridge University Press.

Carroll, N. (2011). On Some Affective Relations between Audiences and the Characters in Popular Fictions. In A. Coplan and P. Goldie (eds), *Empathy: Philosophical and Psychological Perspectives.* Oxford: Oxford University Press, 162–84.

Carruthers, P. (2006). Review of Simulating Minds: The Philosophy, Psychology, and Neuroscience of Mindreading. *Notre Dame Philosophical Reviews.* Available at: <http://ndpr.nd.edu/news/25164-simulating-minds-the-philosophy-psychology-and-neuroscience-of-mindreading/>.

Chamberlain, N. (1938). *The Times*, 28 September, p. 10.

Clay, Z. and M. Iacoboni (2011). Mirroring Fictional Others. In A. Coplan and P. Goldie (eds), *Empathy: Philosophical and Psychological Perspectives.* Oxford: Oxford University Press, 313–29.

Collingwood, R. G. (1925). *Outlines of a Philosophy of Art.* London: Oxford University Press.

Collingwood, R. G. (1945). *Principles of Art.* Oxford: Oxford University Press.

Collingwood, R. G. (1946). *The Idea of History.* Oxford: Clarendon Press.

Collingwood, R. G. (1978). *An Autobiography*. Oxford: Oxford University Press.

Collingwood, R. G. (1999). *The Principles of History: And Other Writings in Philosophy of History*. Oxford: Oxford University Press.

Coplan, A. (2004). Empathic Engagement with Narrative Fictions. *The Journal of Aesthetics and Art Criticism* 62(2): 141–52.

Coplan, A. (2011). Understanding Empathy: Its Features and Effects. In A. Coplan and P. Goldie (eds), *Empathy: Philosophical and Psychological Perspectives*. Oxford: Oxford University Press, 3–18.

Currie, G. (1990). *The Nature of Fiction*. Cambridge: Cambridge University Press.

Currie, G. (1995). *Image and Mind: Film, Philosophy and Cognitive Science*. Cambridge: Cambridge University Press.

Currie, G. (2011). Empathy for Objects. In A. Coplan and P. Goldie (eds), *Empathy: Philosophical and Psychological Perspectives*. Oxford: Oxford University Press, 82–95.

Damasio, A. R. (1996). *Descartes' Error*. London: Papermac.

Davidson, D. (1963). Actions, Reasons, and Causes. *Essays on Actions and Events*. Oxford: Oxford University Press, 3–20.

Davidson, D. (1970). Mental Events. *Essays on Actions and Events*. Oxford: Clarendon Press, 207–25.

Davies, M. and T. Stone (1995). Introduction. *Folk Psychology: The Theory of Mind Debate*. Oxford: Blackwell, 1–44.

Davies, S. (2011). Infectious Music: Music-Listener Emotional Contagion. In A. Coplan and P. Goldie (eds), *Empathy: Philosophical and Psychological Perspectives*. Oxford: Oxford University Press, 134–48.

de Sousa, R. (2014). Emotion. *Stanford Encyclopedia of Philosophy* (spring edn), ed. E. N. Zalta. Available at: <http://plato.stanford.edu/archives/spr2014/entries/emotion/>.

Decety, J., S. Echols and J. Correll (2010). The Blame Game: The Effect of Responsibility and Social Stigma on Empathy for Pain. *The Journal of Cognitive Neuroscience* 22(5): 985–97.

Descartes, R. (1970). Meditations on First Philosophy. In E. M. Anscombe and P. Geach (eds), *Descartes: Philosophical Writings*. London: Nelson, 59–124.

Dilthey, W. (1979). *Selected Writings*. Cambridge: Cambridge University Press.

Dorsch, F. (2012). *The Unity of Imagining*. Frankfurt: Ontos Verlag.

Dray, W. H. (1999). *History as Re-Enactment: R. G. Collingwood's Idea of History*. Oxford: Oxford University Press.

Dumas, A. (1974). *The Three Musketeers*. London: Pan Books.

Eisenberg, N., R. A. Fabes, P. A. Miller, J. Fultz, R. Shell, R. M. Mathy, and R. R. Reno (1989). Relation of Sympathy and

Personal Distress to Prosocial Behaviour: A Multimethod Study. *Journal of Personality and Social Psychology* 57: 55–66.

Feagin, S. L. (1996). *Reading with Feeling*. Ithaca, NY: Cornell University Press.

Feagin, S. L. (2011). Empathizing as Simulating. In A. Coplan and P. Goldie (eds), *Empathy: Philosophical and Psychological Perspectives*. Oxford: Oxford University Press, 149–61.

Fitzgerald, F. S. (2005). *Tender is the Night*. London: The Folio Society.

Forster, M., ed. (2002). *Herder: Philosophical Writings*. Cambridge: Cambridge University Press.

Goldie, P. (2000). *The Emotions*. Oxford: Clarendon Press.

Goldie, P. (2011). Anti-Empathy. In A. Coplan and P. Goldie (eds), *Empathy: Philosophical and Psychological Perspectives*. Oxford: Oxford University Press, 302–17.

Goldman, A. I. (2006). *Simulating Minds: The Philosophy, Psychology, and Neuroscience of Mindreading*. Oxford: Oxford University Press.

Gordon, R. M. (1986). Folk Psychology as Simulation. In M. Davies and T. Stone (eds), *Folk Psychology: The Theory of Mind Debate*. Oxford: Blackwell, 60–73.

Gordon, R. M. (1992). The Simulation Theory: Objections and Misconceptions. In M. Davies and T. Stone (eds), *Folk Psychology: The Theory of Mind Debate*. Oxford: Blackwell, 100–22.

Griswold, C. L. (2006). Imagination, Morals, Science, and Arts. In K. Haakonssen (ed.), *The Cambridge Companion to Adam Smith*. Cambridge: Cambridge University Press, 21–56.

Guyer, P. (2014). *A History of Modern Aesthetics* (Volume 2). Cambridge: Cambridge University Press.

Heal, J. (1986). Replication and Functionalism. *Mind, Reason, and Imagination*. Cambridge: Cambridge University Press, 11–27.

Heal, J. (1988). Co-Cognition and Off-Line Simulation: Two Ways of Understanding the Simulation Approach. *Mind, Reason and Imagination*. Cambridge: Cambridge University Press, 91–114.

Heal, J. (1996a). Simulation and Cognitive Penetrability. *Mind, Reason and Imagination*. Cambridge: Cambridge University Press, 63–88.

Heal, J. (1996b). Simulation, Theory and Content. *Mind, Reason and Imagination*. Cambridge: Cambridge University Press, 45–62.

Heal, J. (1998). Understanding Other Minds from the Inside. *Mind, Reason and Imagination*. Cambridge: Cambridge University Press, 28–44.

Heal, J. (2010). Critical Notice of Alvin Goldman's Simulating Minds. *Philosophical and Phenomenological Research* 80(3): 723–32.

Heal, J. (2013). Social Anti-Individualism, Co-Cognitivism, and Second Person Authority. *Mind* 122: 339–71.

Hempel, C. G. (1962). Explanation in Science and in History. In R. G. Colodney (ed.), *Frontiers of Science and Philosophy*. Pittsburgh, PA: University of Pittsburgh Press, 9–33.

Hempel, C. G. (1966). *Philosophy of Natural Science*. Englewood Cliffs, NJ: Prentice Hall.

Herder, J. G. v. (1774). This Too a Philosophy of History for the Formation of Humanity. In M. Forster (ed.), *Herder: Philosophical Writings*. Cambridge: Cambridge University Press, 272–360.

Herder, J. G. v. (1778). On the Cognition and Sensation of the Human Soul. In M. Forster (ed.), *Johann Gottfried von Herder: Philosophical Writings*. Cambridge: Cambridge University Press, 187–246.

Hoffman, M. L. (2000). *Empathy and Moral Development: Implications for Caring and Justice*. Cambridge: Cambridge University Press.

Hoffman, M. L. (2011). Empathy, Justice, and the Law. In A. Coplan and P. Goldie (eds), *Empathy: Philosophical and Psychological Perspectives*. Oxford: Oxford University Press, 230–54.

Hulme, T. E. (1924). *Speculations: Essays on Humanism and the Philosophy of Art*. London: Kegan Paul, Trench, Trubner, and Co. Ltd.

Hume, D. (1739–40). *A Treatise of Human Nature*. London: Thomas Longman.

Hume, D. (1902). *Enquiries Concerning the Human Understanding and Concerning the Principles of Morals*. Oxford: Clarendon Press.

Hutto, D. D. (2008). *Folk Psychological Narratives: The Sociocultural Basis of Understanding Reasons*. Cambridge, MA: The MIT Press.

Innes, M. (1946). *From London Far*. Harmondsworth: Penguin.

Jahoda, G. (2005). Theodore Lipps and the Shift From "Sympathy" to "Empathy." *Journal of the History of Behavioral Sciences* 41(2): 151–63.

Jamison, L. (2014). *The Empathy Exams* (Kindle). London: Granta Books.

Kahneman, D. and A. Tversky (1982). A Simulation Heuristic. In D. Kahneman and A. Tversky, *Judgement Under Uncertainty: Heuristics and Biases*. Cambridge: Cambridge University Press, 201–8.

Kant, I. (1987). *The Critique of Judgement*. Indianapolis, IN: Hackett.

Kieran, M. (2003). In Search of a Narrative. In M. Kieran and D. M. Lopes (eds), *Imagination, Philosophy, and the Arts*. London: Routledge, 69–87.

Krznaric, R. (2014). *Empathy: A Handbook for Revolution* (Kindle). London: Random House.

Lanzoni, S. (2009). Practicing Psychology in the Art Gallery: Vernon Lee's Aesthetics of Empathy. *The History of the Behavioral Sciences* 45(4): 330–54.

Lee, V. and C. Anstruther-Thomson (1912). *Beauty and Ugliness: And Other Studies in Psychological Aesthetics.* London: John Lane, The Bodley Head.

Lewis, D. (1972). Psychophysical and Theoretical Identifications. *Australasian Journal of Philosophy* 50: 249–58.

Lipps, T. (1903). "Empathy," Inward Imitation, and Sense Feelings. In E. F. Carritt (ed.), *Philosophies of Beauty: From Socrates to Robert Bridges being the Sources of Aesthetic Theory.* Oxford: Clarendon Press, 252–6.

Lipps, T. (1907). Das Wissen from fremden Ich. *Psychologische Untersuchungen.* Leipzig: Engelmann. I: 694–722.

Lopes, D. M. (2011). An Empathic Eye. In A. Coplan and P. Goldie (eds), *Empathy: Philosophical and Psychological Perspectives.* Oxford: Oxford University Press, 118–33.

MacAskill, W. (2015). *Doing Good Better: Effective Altruism and a Radical New Way to Make a Difference.* (Kindle). London: Faber & Faber.

McFee, G. (2011). Empathy: Interpersonal vs. Artistic? In A. Coplan and P. Goldie (eds), *Empathy: Philosophical and Psychological Perspectives.* Oxford: Oxford University Press, 185–208.

Maibom, H. L. (2014). Introduction. In H. L. Maibom (eds), *Empathy and Morality.* Oxford: Oxford University Press, 1–40.

Mallgrave, H. F. and E. Ikonomou, eds. (1994). *Empathy, Form, and Space: Problems in German Aesthetics, 1873–1893.* Los Angeles, CA: Getty Research Institute.

Marr, D. (1982). *Vision: A Computational Investigation into the Human Representation and Processing of Visual Information.* New York: W.H. Freeman and Company.

Matravers, D. (2014). *Fiction and Narrative.* Oxford: Oxford University Press.

Matthew, C., ed. (1997). *Brief Lives: 150 Intimate Biographies of the Famous by the Famous.* Oxford: Oxford University Press.

Meskin, A. and J. M. Weinberg (2006). Imagine That! In M. Kieran, *Contemporary Debates in Aesthetics and the Philosophy of Art.* Oxford: Blackwell, 222–35.

Nichols, S. and S. Stich (1998). Rethinking Co-Cognition: A Reply to Heal. *Mind and Language* 13(4): 499–512.

Nichols, S. and S. Stich (2003). *Mindreading: An Integrated Account of Pretence, Self-Awareness, and Understanding Other Minds.* Oxford: Oxford University Press.

Nichols, S., S. Stich, A. Leslie and D. Klein (1996). Varieties of Off-Line Simulation. In P. Carruthers and P. K. Smith (eds), *Theories of Theories of Mind*. Cambridge: Cambridge University Press, 39–74.

Orwell, G. (2004). *1984*. London: Penguin.

Perry, J. (1979). The Problem of the Essential Indexical. *Nous* 13: 3–21.

Prinz, J. (2011). Is Empathy Necessary for Morality? In A. Coplan and P. Goldie (eds), *Empathy: Philosophical and Psychological Perspectives*. Oxford: Oxford University Press, 211–29.

Rizzolatti, G. and C. Sinigaglia (2008). *Mirrors in the Brain: How Our Minds Share Actions, Emotions, and Experience*. Oxford: Oxford University Press.

Ryle, G. (1963). *The Concept of Mind*. Harmondsworth: Penguin.

Salmela, M. (2012). Shared Emotions. *Philosophical Explorations* 15(1): 33–46.

Schelling, T. (1968). The Life You Save May Be Your Own. In S. Chase (ed.), *Problems in Public Expenditure Analysis*. Washington, DC: The Brookings Institute, 127–62.

Scherner, K. A. (1861). *Das Leben des Traums*. Berlin: Verlag von Heinrich Schindler.

Sherman, G. D. and J. Haidt (2011). Cuteness and Disgust: The Humanizing and Dehumanizing Effects of Emotion. *Emotion Review* 3(3): 1–7.

Singer, P. (1972). Famine, Affluence, and Morality. *Philosophy and Public Affairs* 1(3): 229–43.

Singer, P. (1997). The Drowning Child and the Expanding Circle. *New Internationalist Magazine*. Available at: <https://newint.org/features/1997/04/05/drowning/>.

Slote, M. (2007). *The Ethics of Care and Empathy*. London: Routledge.

Smith, A. (2002). *The Theory of Moral Sentiments*. Cambridge: Cambridge University Press.

Smith, J. (2015) What Is Empathy For? *Synthese* DOI: DOI 10.1007/s1 1229-015-0771-8.

Smith, M. (2011). Empathy, Expansionism, and the Extended Mind. In A. Coplan and P. Goldie (eds), *Empathy: Philosophical and Psychological Perspectives*. Oxford: Oxford University Press, 99–117.

Sober, E. and D. Sloan Wilson (1999). *Unto Others: Evolution and Psychology of Unselfish Behavior*. Cambridge, MA: Harvard University Press.

Stich, S. and S. Nichols (1992). Folk Psychology: Simulation or Tacit Theory? In M. Davies and T. Stone (eds), *Folk Psychology: The Theory of Mind Debate*. Oxford: Blackwell, 123–58.

Stich, S. and S. Nichols (1997). Cognitive Penetrability, Rationality, and Restricted Simulation. *Mind and Language* 12: 297–326.

Stock, K. (2011). Unpacking the Boxes: The Cognitive Theory of Imagination and Aesthetics. In E. Schellekens and P. Goldie (eds), *The Aesthetic Mind: Philosophy and Psychology*. Oxford: Oxford University Press, 268–82.

Stueber, K. R. (2006). *Rediscovering Empathy: Agency, Folk Psychology, and the Human Sciences*. Cambridge, MA: MIT Press.

Titchener, E. (1909). *Lectures on the Experimental Psychology of the Thought-Processes*. New York: Macmillan.

Underwood, B. and B. Moore (1982). Perspective Taking and Altruism. *Psychological Bulletin* 91: 43–73.

Vischer, R. (1873). On the Optical Sense of Form: A Contribution to Aesthetics. In H. F. Mallgrave and E. Ikonomou (eds), *Empathy, Form and Space: Problems in German Aesthetics, 1873–1893*. Los Angeles, CA: Getty Research Institute, 90–124.

Walton, K. (1990). *Mimesis as Make-Believe*. Cambridge, MA: Harvard University Press.

Walton, K. L. (1999). Projectivism, Empathy, and Musical Tension. *In Other Shoes: Music, Metaphor, Empathy, Existence*. Oxford: Oxford University Press, 118–50.

Walton, K. (2015). Empathy, Imagination, and Phenomenal Concepts. *In Other Shoes: Music, Metaphor, Empathy, Existence*. Oxford: Oxford University Press, 1–16.

Williams, B. (1966). Imagination and the Self. *Problems of the Self*. Cambridge: Cambridge University Press, 26–45.

Williams, B. (1973a). Consequentialism and Integrity. In S. Scheffler (ed.), *Consequentialism and Its Critics*. Oxford: Oxford University Press, 20–50.

Williams, B. (1973b). Egoism and Altruism. *Problems of the Self*. Cambridge: Cambridge University Press, 250–65.

Williams, B. (1985). *Ethics and the Limits of Philosophy*. London: Fontana.

Wollheim, R. (1979). The Sheep and the Ceremony. *The Mind and Its Depths*. Cambridge, MA: Harvard University Press, 1–21.

Wollheim, R. (1986). *The Thread of Life*. Cambridge: Cambridge University Press.

Wollheim, R. (1987). *Painting as an Art*. London: Thames and Hudson.

Wollheim, R. (1991). Correspondence, Projective Properties and Expression in the Arts. *The Mind and its Depths*. Cambridge, MA: Harvard University Press, 144–58.

Woolf, V. (1927). *To the Lighthouse*. New York: Harcourt, Brace & World.

Index